Six Keys to
Buddhist
Living

Six Keys to
Buddhist
Living

Simple rules for joy and peace of mind

MADONNA GAUDING

A GODSFIELD BOOK
www.godsfieldpress.com

This book is dedicated to my teacher,
Gehlek Rimpoche

First published in Great Britain in 2005 by Godsfield Press,
a division of Octopus Publishing Group Ltd
2–4 Heron Quays
London E14 4JP

Distributed in the United States and Canada by
Sterling Publishing Co., Inc.
387 Park Avenue South, New York, NY 10016-8810

10 9 8 7 6 5 4 3 2 1

Printed and bound in China

ISBN 1-84181-252-8
EAN 9781841812526

Contents

INTRODUCTION

In 1969 the soulful singing legend Peggy Lee won a Grammy for her hit song *Is that all there is?* The answer the Buddha would have given, had he been in the audience, is 'No, definitely not!' He taught that, with some effort, we can overhaul our view of the world and 'get a life'. That is, we can have a life that is more satisfying and happy than we ever dreamed. We can become enlightened, and free ourselves from all suffering and negativity. At the most profound level, the Buddha taught that love and compassion — cherishing others as much as ourself — and developing personal wisdom, are the ultimate keys to happiness.

No matter what our spiritual or religious beliefs, we all want to be enlightened. We all want to love fully, to feel unlimited compassion and to live with an open heart. But despite our best intentions, we hold back when we want to be generous; we get angry and judge others when we would prefer to be tolerant and patient. We then try to justify our aggressive behaviour, knowing it isn't how we really want to be. Our shortsightedness and our negative patterns keep us locked in a rut of unhappiness. It is as if we are continually driving east when we want to go west. We instinctively know we're on the wrong road, but we don't have a map to lead us in the right direction.

The good news is that the Buddha gave us a road map to happiness that we can rely on. You don't have to be a Buddhist to benefit from his excellent advice — his teachings complement all spiritual traditions. And if you don't practise any particular path, that's OK, too.

The Buddha was an exceedingly happy person who embodied love and compassion. But he didn't achieve this state without concentrated effort. He

had to work to change his negative habits into positive ones. His teachings show us how he transformed himself from an ordinary human who was sometimes mean, angry and lazy, had problems concentrating, a wavering morality and a limited, materialistic view of life, into a fully enlightened, infinitely loving and compassionate buddha. His Six Keys highlight the ways in which he overcame his weaknesses and achieved enlightenment. The first four are focused outwardly, on others, whereas the last two specifically help you to develop yourself. Consider the Buddha's Keys, set out below, as six simple rules for happy living.

1 **Let it go.** Be generous to yourself and others

2 **Do no harm.** Honour your commitments and act with compassion

3 **Bite your tongue.** Control your anger and banish self-hate

4 **Sweat it out.** Approach life with enthusiasm and perseverance

5 **Stick to the point.** Learn to focus and concentrate your mind

6 **Get real.** Life is more vast and profound than you can imagine.

The keys are not moralistic rules designed to keep you in your place. They're offered as a joyful means to liberate yourself from suffering. The Buddha simply encouraged us to try them, and judge for ourselves whether they are helpful or not.

BUDDHA'S BASICS

The Buddha taught the keys in the context of four basic truths: karma, reincarnation, the interconnectedness of all life and impermanence. As these concepts may be new to you, let's begin with some brief explanations.

WHAT GOES AROUND COMES AROUND

The Buddha taught the laws of karma: the principle that everything you do or think creates a positive, negative or neutral result. In other words, your experience today is the result of your past thoughts and actions. You can see karma in action in your daily life. If you're a negative and angry person, you create negative experience — for yourself and those around you. If you're a positive and loving person, your life will be more positive generally. It's easy to believe that external forces shape your reality, but most often, it is your own mind and actions that determine your experience of life. The keys help you generate positive karma.

HOW MANY TIMES DO WE GO ROUND?

The Buddha also taught reincarnation: the belief that your life force in its most subtle form does not die but is reborn into another life. The keys help you live a happy life and also ensure a positive future life. You may believe in an afterlife, or you may believe that when you die you simply cease to exist. When working with the keys, try to keep an open mind about the possibility of your own rebirth. Doing so will give you an enhanced sense of responsibility, a larger perspective on reality and a more relaxed view of your current life. Instead of feeling that you only have one chance, you'll see yourself as a work-in-progress, with the opportunity to evolve spiritually from one life to the next.

YOU'RE NOT ALONE

It is hard to be happy if you believe you are separate and alone. You *are* an individual, but you're also embedded in and intimately interconnected with the entire universe. What you think, do and say affects everyone and everything else. A contemporary Buddhist teacher, Thich Nhat Han, calls this reality 'InterBeing'. When you work with the keys, remember that you are a part of the great web of life. When you are generous towards or patient with others, you cannot help but benefit yourself.

NOTHING STAYS THE SAME

Life is change. You're not the same from one minute to the next, and neither is anyone or anything else. When working with the keys, it helps to realize that nothing is permanent. You may have difficulty working with their teachings on one day, but have an entirely wonderful experience the next. Accepting impermanence enables you let go of the past and embrace the present, knowing you have infinite capacity to change and evolve for the better. It helps you to stop clinging to people, possessions or that great time you had at the beach yesterday. It enables you to cherish the moment and live your life to the fullest.

THE KEYS IN COMBINATION

Each key relies on the others in order to work well. For instance, in order to be truly generous you have to **Let it go**. You **Do no harm** by giving appropriately and choosing something you acquired honestly and ethically. If the person you gifted is ungrateful, you **Bite your tongue** and disallow any anger or disappointment. By letting go of any 'strings' or expectations attached to your gift, you slowly build your love and compassion, which creates energy and inspires further enthusiastic effort and perseverance. You **Sweat it out** over time and become even more generous, loving and compassionate. Through your enthusiastic efforts you naturally improve your focus and concentration, and develop your ability to **Stick to the point** in all that you do. You then apply your improved concentration to meditation. You **Get real** by contemplating the meaning of your life and the true nature of your reality. You begin to understand what it is to be wise. If you work long and hard, you will eventually achieve enlightenment. At the very least, you will become much happier and more content.

HOW TO USE THIS BOOK

Each chapter opens with an introduction to one of the six keys. The rest of the chapter provides more in-depth explanations, exercises, guided meditations and visualizations, all designed to help you make the key a part of your life. Although reading about the keys is important, it's through daily practice and contemplation that you reap their benefits. Try to work through the book from start to finish, rather than dip in and out, as each key builds on what has been learned before. Keep a journal of your experience and insights as you progress.

Welcome to the Buddha's Keys, a guide to opening your heart and living a happier life.

KEY **1**

LET IT GO

The truth is that it hurts to hold on and feels good to let go. The Buddha taught that showing generosity brings you abundant joys and benefits, both in this life and the next. If you can get into the habit of giving away money and material possessions, you'll gradually reduce your attachment to them. Parting with your money will lessen its emphasis in your life; giving away your 'stuff' will reduce the stress and anxiety that comes with storing, managing and maintaining the mountain of things we all tend to accumulate. Your acts of generosity will help you to restore balance and perspective, allowing you to focus on the things that matter in life — love, family, friends and experience.

But we have much more to give than money and possessions. There's great joy to be found in giving knowledge and emotional support. Give away your knowledge and you'll free yourself of that constricting, competitive mindset. Share your spiritual wisdom and you in turn will feel blessed and supported. When you help relieve others of their fear, you heal your own soul as well.

When you practise this first key, start slowly and honour your limits. Only give what you can give comfortably. Begin by reading more about generosity in this chapter, try the exercises and practise the guided meditations. Keep notes

to see how your life and mood improves on a day-to-day basis, as your

capacity to give expands and increases over time. The point of practising

generosity, according to the Buddha, is to help generate love and compassion

for yourself and all other beings. Generosity brings such joy and happiness,

you'll soon find yourself looking for opportunities to give.

THREE KINDS OF GENEROSITY

The Buddha taught not one but three forms of generosity, and almost every generous act you can think of falls into one of his categories. You practise the first form of generosity when you give money and material goods, and also your time. The second and third forms of generosity are less obvious: giving protection from fear, and sharing spiritual and other knowledge.

MATERIAL GENEROSITY

Let's begin with the easiest type of generosity to understand and practise. You can make a good start by donating a small amount of money to a charity, perhaps one that helps children, animals or the environment. Pick one that touches your heart. Or decide to give a little more in your weekly donation to church, synagogue, mosque or temple. Consider what possessions you have and don't use, and be willing to give them away if someone else needs them.

Check your motivation. Before you give materially, ask yourself why you are giving. Try to give without agenda. In other words, try not to give

THINGS TO DO

Buy a bowlful of organic fruit. Go to work early and place it in the communal area of your workspace for everyone to share. Don't let anyone know that you are the giver. Notice the reaction of your fellow workers. How does it feel to give without recognition, simply for the joy of making those around you happy?

in order to encourage someone to like you or to make someone feel indebted. If you are giving publicly, try not to look for recognition or praise for your philanthropy. Instead, try to give from your heart, with a genuine desire to support others and help relieve their suffering.

Don't underestimate the power of small gifts. Be creative and practise a small form of material generosity on a daily basis, no matter how insignificant it may seem. Each act builds your capacity to give, loosens your attachment to your money and possessions, and increases your happiness and that of those around you. Make a little extra soup on a cold day and share it with your neighbour, or give some change to that homeless person you pass every day on the street. After a period of time, you may be able to give substantially, perhaps by making a gift of an expensive possession, or giving monetary help to someone in serious need. No matter how small or extravagant your gifts, practising generosity every day will change you, and the world, for the better.

Time is money

Even if you don't have money or possessions to give away, you can still practise the first form of generosity. You could donate some of your time and labour to caring for the sick or elderly. Try volunteering to be a children's tutor or teach adults who need to learn to read. Or volunteer at a hospice and help people die with as much dignity and peace as possible. Spend time doing house repairs and maintenance for an elderly couple in your community who

THINGS TO DO

Make a list of things you could do to help others that don't involve money or possessions. Here are some suggestions to get you started:

- Pick up litter in your local park or nature area
- Drive elderly people to their doctor appointments
- Tutor children after school
- Teach a friend how to use a computer
- Give a massage
- Visit someone who's sick
- Cook a meal for an overworked relative
- Volunteer at your local church, library, school or hospital
- Donate your time at an animal shelter

can no longer handle the work. Work with an environmental group in your area. The opportunities to give some of your time and energy are endless. With practice and the right motivation, you'll find yourself giving more freely every day, with great joy and without reservation or regret.

GIVING REASSURANCE, SUPPORT AND PROTECTION

This second form of generosity involves giving help and aid to people who suffer from any kind of fear or anxiety — which includes most people on our planet. Consider how many of us have fears about our health, our relationships or paying our bills. When you practise this form of generosity, you make yourself available to talk with and comfort friends, family members and even strangers.

Spend extra time with your spouse or children when their fears and anxieties get the best of them. If you have a relative or friend who is chronically angry, look deeper and you may discover that what they are really feeling is fear. If they constantly judge you, it may be because they are afraid of their own inadequacy. Helping people understand how their anger is covering up their fear helps them cope with both. By helping protect people from their own fear, you create a more peaceful world for us all.

Fear can become a habit or a way of viewing the world. It may have its roots in a difficult childhood. If you want to help a friend who is stuck in fear mode, encourage them to broaden their view, relax and see that living can be joyful and fun. Open them to the idea of practising generosity in their own life. Distract them from their preoccupation with what negative things may happen, and help them learn to 'smell the roses'. If you have a tendency to be fearful yourself, helping a friend can heal your own fear.

Giving support to those facing real difficulty

You may know someone who has good reason to be fearful. Perhaps the company they work for is planning redundancies and they are afraid of losing their job, or a routine blood test shows an abnormality and they are afraid of what it could mean. You can help in these situations by being generous with your time and attention. Be willing to listen and, if asked, help with problem solving and decision making.

When you practise generosity towards someone who is suffering from fear, be very sensitive to that person's needs. Try to let go of any desire to feel wanted or appreciated. Don't imagine yourself as a superhero, swooping in to rescue the day. A person who is frightened needs someone to listen, to help them gain perspective, or make decisions in a difficult situation. He or she may need practical as well as emotional support. Help the person find their own strength, and take your cues from them so that you can be genuinely helpful.

Giving protection to those suffering from trauma

You may come into contact with someone who has experienced a traumatic event — perhaps a natural disaster, such as a hurricane, tornado, flood or a fire. Or you may know someone who has recently returned from serving in a war zone as a soldier or volunteer. By supporting people who are recovering from such extreme experience, you're practising generosity.

Whenever large-scale tragedies or natural disasters occur, a volunteer or church group is invariably organized to provide help. In these circumstances, you have an excellent opportunity to be generous with your time and labour, and to give monetary and material support. You may be able to help by filling sandbags to protect homes during a flood, for example, or by making sandwiches for rescue workers, or easing the anxieties and fears of children whose lives are in upheaval.

Animals are sentient beings, too

The Buddha taught love and compassion for all sentient beings. By 'all sentient beings' he meant all the living beings that inhabit the universe, including animals, birds and insects. If you are an animal lover, try practising generosity by volunteering at an animal rescue centre. Providing abused animals with protection from fear is a great way to open your heart. Rescue organizations exist for horses, dogs, cats, birds, farm animals of all kinds, and even exotic animals like tigers, lions and alligators.

THINGS TO DO

Buddhists have a special practice of, one day a year, rescuing animals and freeing them into the wild. You can practise this yourself by buying live fish or worms from a fishing shop and releasing them in a stream or wood. Say a prayer for their wellbeing as you practise the generosity of extending their life.

GIVING SPIRITUAL AND PRACTICAL KNOWLEDGE

The third form of generosity the Buddha taught is to give spiritual knowledge. You may feel this is better left to people with some sort of credentials, such as the clergy, but we have all learned lessons from life, and gained wisdom from our spiritual traditions, or the many teachers we have encountered. With the right motivation and sensitivity, you can share your spiritual knowledge directly with friends and family. Instead of talking about nothing at dinner, try moving the conversation in a more meaningful direction. With an intention to be helpful, share what is spiritually important to you, then give your attention to what others have to share. You could start a conversation about generosity, for instance, and how you're trying to improve your ability to give. You can also share your spiritual knowledge through your creativity as an artist, a performer, a writer or a musician.

Sharing practical or technical knowledge is another important form of generosity. By helping a friend negotiate legal or governmental bureaucracy, for example, you're performing a great service. Instead of hoarding knowledge at work, share freely and help foster an environment of generosity that will benefit everyone, including yourself.

JOURNAL EXERCISE

Find some time when you can be alone and undisturbed. Your challenge is to write down everything you know. Start with your work skills: list all the things you know how to do and get paid for doing. If you have a lot of academic or other training, list that too. Then move on to other skills. Perhaps you're a good cook or know how to restore furniture. Maybe you're handy with computers or know a lot about alternative health care. Next, write down your less obvious gifts, such as being able to spot a great deal in a thrift shop.

Once you have listed your practical skills, spend some time writing down all that you know about the spiritual side of life. This will be harder. Start by writing what you've learned about how to love others. Continue writing about your religious beliefs. Finally, list what you know about the big questions we all ask from time to time: What is my purpose in this life? Who or what is God or my higher power? What happens when I die and what can I do to ensure a good death?

Read over what you've written and take note of just how much knowledge and information you have to share with others. Try to be more open-hearted and generous with what you know, and sensitive about when and how you share it.

TROUBLESHOOTING YOUR GENEROSITY

It's easy to talk about generosity but harder to practise it. Don't be discouraged if you feel mean or selfish instead of open-hearted and giving, or if your efforts to give aren't going smoothly. Your technique probably needs a little troubleshooting.

If you're afraid to be generous, you may have issues from your childhood. Perhaps your family had to scrape to pay the bills, or your early attempts to be generous were disparaged in some way. If you sense that fear is holding you back, explore what's behind it and spend some time clearing out those old ghosts from your past. Then try little experiments in giving while making an effort to stay mentally focused in the present. Keep notes on your progress in your journal.

WHO IS NOT DESERVING?

You often say, 'I would give, but only to the
   deserving.'

The trees in your orchard say not so, nor the flocks in
   your pasture.

They give that they may live, for to withhold is to perish.

Surely he who is worthy to receive his days and his nights, is worthy of
   all else from you.

And he who has deserved to drink from the ocean of life deserves to
   fill his cup from your little stream.

KAHLIL GIBRAN

If you've plunged headlong into giving and your efforts seem to be making things worse rather than better, you may need to be more thoughtful in your approach. Pull back, sit down and think about what's best for the other person. If you are trying to 'fix' someone by signing him or her up for a therapy group against their wishes, your efforts at generosity are misguided. Giving requires sensitivity and wisdom, and the creativity to know how best to help another individual.

If you unconsciously or consciously want something in return for your giving — whether it's affection, love, fame or recognition — your efforts are unlikely to be effective or rewarding. If you give in order to make someone dependent on you, your generosity is nothing more than a form of control. On the other hand, if you give without manipulation or agenda, you'll free yourself from the stress of expectations and the disappointment when these aren't met. If you give to help relieve suffering and create happiness, your generosity will be truly loving and compassionate.

PRACTISING EQUANIMITY

Who is deserving of your generosity? The Buddha taught that you should give to ten different kinds of people: enemies, friends and those you haven't made up your mind about; the ethical and the unethical; your equals, inferiors and superiors; those who are helpful and happy, and those who are harmful and angry. That just about covers everybody — which stands on its head any idea that only certain people are worthy of generosity.

This is where the Buddha's basics (see page 8) come in to play. If everyone is reincarnated, then the person you find it hard to give to today may have been your beloved partner in a former life. Even within this lifetime, you may find someone difficult now but fall in love with him or her in the future. How often does a best friend turn into a worst enemy or a despised enemy transform into a beloved friend? The next time the person at work you can't stand has a birthday, be the first to donate for his or her present.

Because we are all connected, no matter who receives our generosity, we're helping ourselves as well. If you practise equanimity — the ability to give to friends, enemies and strangers alike — you'll lessen your feelings of anger and judgment and you'll find you're much more accepting of yourself because of it. As you stretch your self and give to those you would normally exclude, your heart will grow along with your ability to give.

MEDITATING ON GENEROSITY

As well as practising generosity, it's also important to meditate on this first key. Sit down in a quiet place where you can be alone and undisturbed. Recall the positive benefits that come from practising generosity. Go over the material in this chapter and add insights of your own. Think about how you feel when you're generous with friends, family, colleagues and even strangers. Do you feel more loving, expansive and relaxed? How do you feel when you're withholding and miserly with yourself and your possessions. Note any resistance you've experienced in your giving and try to understand what is holding you back.

Try the Tibetan Buddhist meditation on the page opposite as part of your contemplation. It's an especially beautiful visualization, and a powerful tool to use to encourage your generosity.

VISUALIZATION

Imagine your body, your virtuous actions and your positive energy transformed into a beautiful, wish-fulfilling tree. This tree is covered with silver and gold and its flowers and fruit are made of precious jewels, such as emeralds, diamonds and rubies. Visualize light radiating from your jewel tree to every corner of the planet. At the tip of every light ray is what every sentient being needs. Imagine that every living thing has all that it requires. Imagine everyone relieved of every fear, however small or devastating. Visualize a world in which everyone has all the practical and spiritual information they need to live their lives in peace and harmony. Hold this loving thought in your mind for a minute or two, then gather back the light to the wish-fulfilling tree and return to your normal self.

EXPRESSING GRATITUDE

If you can be grateful for what you have, you'll conquer your sense of not having enough, and you'll have an easier time being generous with yourself, your money and your possessions. Take a few minutes every day to appreciate the quality of your life — the material comfort you enjoy, the relationships that sustain you and the beauty of the world around you. Try to be satisfied, on a daily basis, with what you have. When you experience that urge to have more and better, take a moment to ask yourself if you really need that new gadget or yet another pair of shoes.

It's very easy in contemporary life to place too much emphasis on money and material goods. Try to focus instead on the intangibles that determine the quality of your life, such as enjoyment of nature, loving relationships, a satisfying work life and spiritual connection. Make an effort to give these intangibles as much importance and attention as money and material possessions. Try to balance the many competing aspects of your life so you don't become lopsided — by working too hard, always going shopping or always socializing. Your newfound balance and sense of what's important in life will combine to make your giving effortless and richly rewarding.

GIVING THANKS MEDITATION

Find a quiet place where you will not be disturbed. Breathe deeply and clear your mind. Try to be focused and present in this moment. Now contemplate the following:

I am blessed with much more than most people on the planet. I have the basic necessities of food, shelter and clothing. I am grateful for having what I need when countless people on our planet don't even have clean water to drink. Not only do I have my basic necessities, I have also had the good fortune to be cared for, supported and protected by many people throughout my life, from the time I was an infant until today. My parents and my relatives, the scores of teachers I've known, the leaders of my spiritual community, the police, firemen and health care workers have all helped me in countless ways.

I have also known lovers, friends, fellow students and colleagues who have benefited me enormously. It's impossible to recall the hundreds, perhaps thousands of people I have encountered who have helped me lead a better life — from shop assistants to librarians, to wonderful people I've met briefly on a bus or plane. And there are people whom I have never met — the farmers who produce the food I eat and countless workers who create the goods I enjoy. I should also not forget the many artists, writers, actors and musicians who have inspired me with their creativity.

As I sit here, I feel extremely blessed with everything I have in my life. I am grateful for what has been given to me, and what I have learned and experienced because of it. I feel enormous gratitude to the givers of these countless blessings, and I am indebted to them beyond what I could ever repay. I aspire to practise generosity on a daily basis, so that others can feel as fortunate as I do today.

After contemplating the above, sit quietly. Visualize the countless people who have helped you standing as a group, in front of you, as far as you can see. Mentally thank them and take responsibility for passing on their generosity to others.

LEARNING TO RECEIVE

The last, but not least, part of being generous is learning how to receive. If you've had a lot of disappointments in the past, you may be closed down to the idea of getting help, receiving gifts or accepting the generosity of others. Sometimes it's easier to give help than to admit you need it yourself. It means letting yourself be vulnerable. But if you can understand how it feels to be on the receiving end of generosity, you'll be much more effective as a giver. You'll not only benefit from the gift, you'll also be helping others practise generosity.

KEY 2

DO NO HARM

This key seems straightforward enough, but there's more to it than meets the eye. First, distinguishing between harmful and harmless actions can be more difficult than you think. Second, just avoiding harmful actions does not make this key a part of your life. Its traditional name is 'Ethical Discipline', which should give you an idea of the work and dedication involved. Why is it worth it? Because living an ethical life is the basis on which you can develop all your other good qualities — it's the 'soil' the other keys grow in. Living a disciplined, ethical life cannot fail but make you a happier person.

Of all the keys, Do no harm has the most potential to be misinterpreted. It isn't about rule keeping and righteousness, or narrow-mindedness and judgment. As long as you do no harm to yourself or others, how you live your life is your business. If you're gay or straight, it makes no difference. You can practise the second key whoever you are: whether you dye your hair orange, live out of a backpack or have a place in the boardroom.

You don't have to live up to the expectations of others or tie yourself up in knots worrying about every thought or action. The idea of the second key is to be relaxed, self-contained and open-minded. When working with the Do no harm principle, you begin to establish a clear set of moral values. With the Buddha's guidance, you can develop a reliable, ethical compass that will guide your life.

Remember the Buddha's basic teachings about interdependence and karma? He taught that everything we think and everything we do affects our life and the lives of others, and that everything we do has a positive or negative consequence. It can be hard to distinguish between what's positive and what's negative, what's harmful and what isn't. This chapter will help you establish what to embrace and what to avoid.

WHY DO WE CAUSE HARM?

If you are causing harm to yourself or others, you are probably under the influence of what the Buddha called 'delusions'. A more modern term might be 'negative emotions'. The Buddha identified hundreds of delusions, but the three principle ones are attachment, anger and ignorance.

The first delusion, attachment, is the source of a great deal of misery. Another name for it is desire — for anything and anyone, be it a new car or a lover. You can also have attachment to intangibles, such as fame or status. It's human to have desire, but becoming overly attached and wanting to possess people or things can provoke any number of negative actions. If you confuse attachment with love, you will seek to possess and control your partner, friend, relative or child, rather than work for their happiness.

The second delusion, anger, is the fuel for a range of abusive behaviour. Hatred is its close cousin. Its by-product is violence: anger leads to wars between and within nations. It closes down your heart and distorts your thinking.

VISUALIZATION

Find a few minutes in the morning when you can be alone. Think of what you have planned for the day. Perhaps you're going to work, taking care of the children or running errands. Now, imagine that everything you do during the next 24 hours will be positive and uplifting for yourself and everyone with whom you come into contact. If that's not possible, then at the very least imagine that you will do no harm to yourself or anyone else. Try to keep this intention in mind throughout your day.

If you suffer from the third delusion, ignorance, you haven't realized that your actions have a consequence, or that you're connected to all living beings. You may deny any future life, and focus all your energies to getting ahead in the moment. You may see no reason for spiritual development and have no desire to understand your true nature or the true nature of reality.

Everyone struggles with the delusions of attachment, anger and ignorance, and we cause ourselves and others pain on their account. The Buddha knew from personal experience how devastating their effects can be. Before he became enlightened he struggled with delusions himself. In fact, in the moments preceding his enlightenment, he had his most intense struggle. Without exercising judgement and with great compassion born from his personal experience, he shared the methods he discovered for overcoming them. But first, let's look at a simple way you can categorize your actions to determine which are positive and which will have a negative effect, both for yourself and others.

THREE CATEGORIES OF ACTION

All our actions can be broadly divided into three categories. You can work out what category an action belongs to by assessing your level of happiness when carrying it out and your motivation.

First, there are those actions that result in both your immediate and ultimate happiness. Practising wholehearted generosity is a good example. Thinking and meditating about love and compassion is another. Not only are these actions personally rewarding, they also contribute to your eventual future enlightenment. In an ideal world, all your actions would fall into this first category.

Second, there are those actions that cause you and others unhappiness, both now and in the future. Being abusive towards your partner is a typical example, as is plotting revenge against someone at work or stealing from your clients by 'cooking the books'. All such actions are bound to cause unhappiness and bring you negative consequences in this life and the next. Actions of this kind are very often fuelled by anger, attachment and ignorance. They are usually easy to identify as negative which, in theory, makes them easy to avoid.

Third are those actions that bring you short-lived happiness, but generate negative results in the long term. At first glance, these actions may not seem negative, which makes them difficult to resist. Any dieter knows this one.

You can justify eating chocolate cake and ice cream because it tastes so good. But if you're already overweight, you'll pay for your actions in increased girth and worsening health. Another good example is having an affair when you're in a committed relationship. The romance may be exciting and pleasurable, but the longer-term consequence is pain for all involved. Many of our actions fall into this third category — and they're motivated mainly by attachment and ignorance. It's true that these actions bring happiness for a while, but they don't deliver the goods in terms of ultimate happiness or enlightenment.

THINGS TO DO

Many great Tibetan Buddhist teachers have used white and black stones to keep track of their positive and negative actions. Find or buy some to use yourself. Before you go to bed, think of what you did during the day. When you recall a positive and beneficial action, place a white stone in front of you. When you recall an action that was negative or questionable, place a black stone to the left of it. Continue adding to your piles of stones as you rerun your day. When you finish, note which pile is larger. Try to reduce the number of your black stones and increase the amount of white stones a little more every day.

THE BUDDHA'S TEN COMMANDMENTS

Now you have some guidelines regarding categories of action, let's look at what the Buddha considered the ten negative, or non-virtuous actions to avoid. The list has a lot in common with the Ten Commandments of the Judeo-Christian tradition, except the Buddha didn't command anyone to do anything; he only pointed out activities it is wise to avoid. From his enlightened perspective, the Buddha knew these actions create bad karma or negative energy, and will only cause you and others to suffer and be unhappy. He further divided his list into actions of body, speech and thought.

Being a realistic and compassionate person, the Buddha understood that until you are enlightened and free from all negativity, you won't be able to avoid these ten actions completely. He suggested instead that we become aware of them, work to avoid them and practise virtuous acts in their place. Doing so, he taught, will move you along the road to complete happiness and becoming a buddha yourself.

HARMFUL ACTIONS OF THE BODY

Killing

You may feel this one has no relevance in your life, but the Buddha had a broad view. Included in this non-virtuous action is a request to cut down or eliminate the killing of animals and insects. We all kill insects, even if only inadvertently, while walking, driving or gardening. If you eat meat, you are indirectly or directly participating in killing animals, fish and birds. It may be unrealistic for you to

avoid killing altogether, but you can become more conscious of the suffering of other species. This will help you to become a more sensitive and compassionate person.

Antidote actions: If you are an activist, join a group dedicated to ending war and promoting peace. Try eating less meat or becoming a vegetarian. When insects or mice appear in your home, instead of killing them, catch them and release them outdoors.

Stealing

The idea of stealing anything from anyone may appall you. However, you may be taking from others without fully realizing it, through manipulation. For example, you may tell your grandmother how much you admire her flower vase, because you want to encourage her to give it to you. Or you may steal through your business by padding your invoice or by cheating on your taxes or insurance claims. Try to maintain respect for the right of others to their own property.

Antidote actions: Adopt fair and ethical business practices. Be willing to pay more for goods so people can make a fair wage. Whenever you have a desire to take something from someone, give something to that person instead.

Sexual misconduct

You know you're guilty of sexual misconduct if your behaviour in this department causes suffering — either to yourself or others. It doesn't have anything to do with who you sleep with or how many sexual partners you enjoy or what you do in bed. Try to avoid manipulation, coercion or dishonesty in your sexual affairs. If you are heterosexual, be responsible and use birth control. Be vigilant about contacting or spreading sexually transmitted diseases. If you have made a commitment to another person to be faithful, stick to it.

Antidote actions: Try to be a more giving, passionate and compassionate lover. Practise kindness in your sexual affairs.

HARMFUL ACTIONS OF SPEECH

Lying

The question is not whether you tell lies, but how often. Everyone lies. You may find it more relevant to ask yourself how often you stretch the truth. It's easy to say something false to appease someone, exaggerate your sales figures to impress your boss, inflate your credentials to get a job or flatter your date to make an evening go smoothly. If you're afraid or pushed into a corner, you may well lie blatantly.

Antidote actions: To increase your awareness, keep a journal of how many times a day you stretch the truth or tell an outright lie. Try to minimize your 'truth stretching' and communicate directly and honestly with others.

Divisive speech

By divisive speech, the Buddha meant speaking to someone or a group with the intention of causing disharmony. For example, when you're jealous of someone's friendship with another person, you may be tempted to point out the other person's negative qualities. If you tell a racist or sexist joke at work, you denigrate another religious or ethnic group with the intention of encouraging others to feel the same way. When making a political statement, you may attempt to demonize the opposition. On reflection, you will see that divisive speech harms you as much as it harms others because it can only foster negativity.

Antidote actions: Monitor any tendency you have to judge others and confront any racism or sexism you may be harbouring in your heart and mind. If you have the opportunity to speak in front of a large group, make sure all you say promotes peace and harmony.

Hurtful speech

Speech that is hurtful carries an intention to cause pain. You may shout at someone or speak sweetly and politely — what matters is your desire to hurt. There are so many subtle ways to get a hurtful message across. You want to hurt Bill so you say, 'Bill, your work is great, but have you seen John's report? It's fantastic!' You also practise hurtful speech when you inflict your bad mood on others or stay silent when you know this will cause harm.

Antidote actions: If you're angry with someone, don't speak until you feel you can do so without being hurtful. Try, as best you can, to be kind and supportive in all that you say.

Meaningless speech

The Buddha wasn't suggesting that you don't chat with your friends, tell jokes at a party or exchange pleasantries with your neighbour. His advice is not to waste your time talking about nothing when you could be doing something more productive. The 'something more productive' could include any of the antidote actions listed in this section. The more positive actions you take, the less negativity you will have in your life and the quicker you will become completely happy and free from suffering.

Antidote actions: Be more conscious of how you use your time. Try not to use meaningless chatter and gossip as a means to avoid more productive and positive activities. Consider giving your phone a rest. Cut down on time spent in Internet chat rooms.

HARMFUL ACTIONS OF THOUGHT

Covetous thinking

Advertising is designed to fuel your senses of attachment and desire. Cars, clothes, electronic gadgets, beauty, sexiness and power — it's all for sale, round the clock. Unless you live in a cave, you are constantly bombarded with the message that you must want things. The problem comes when you focus your mind on wanting a particular object and you mentally tell yourself you'll do anything to get it. You can feel this way about a person, too. It's beyond just wanting something: it's becoming obsessed with the idea of having it.

Antidote actions: Meditate on impermanence and how, when you eventually leave this life, you'll leave everything and everyone behind.

Harmful thinking

When you purposefully plan to create obstacles for someone — to give your employee a bad review, for example, because you don't want to give them a pay rise — you generate negative karma. It doesn't matter if you go through with your plan or not. Simply wishing difficulties on another person contributes negative energy to the universe.

Antidote actions: Monitor your thinking and try to intervene when you find yourself wishing bad luck on others.

Wrong view

Holding the wrong view means not accepting that your actions have consequences or that you have a future life. It refers to a mistaken idea of oneself as a solid 'I' that exists separately from the rest of reality, which we shall examine more in our discussion of the sixth key (keep an open mind for now). You are also suffering from having a wrong view if you see spiritual development as pointless and your life as meaningless.

THINGS TO DO

One of the hardest things to do in life is to make a genuine apology. However, it can also be incredibly freeing. If you have harmed someone in the past, and not acknowledged your wrongdoing, now is the time to make amends.

If you don't feel comfortable talking to the person directly, write a letter. Let them know you sincerely regret any harm you've caused them, and ask if there is something you could do to help heal the damage. You may not be ready to send the letter, but the act of writing it alone will help move your mind in a positive direction.

Antidote actions: Recall that spiritual masters throughout the ages and in all traditions have taught that there are profound truths to be discovered and experienced through spiritual practice. If it helps you, read about the discoveries of modern physics for confirmation of some of these ancient truths. It is known that in the sub-atomic world, for instance, particles are not separate, solid entities, but are interconnected. They can also be simultaneously a particle and a wave. Or consider that the flapping of a butterfly's wings in China affects the weather in Europe.

WHAT ABOUT THE GREY AREAS?

The Buddha recognized that a list of non-virtuous actions doesn't provide us with enough guidance to know when we have generated bad karma. He knew that each human act is accompanied by mitigating factors and circumstances. Because of this, he added a postscript to help us understand what is a completely negative act and what is only negative in part.

THINGS TO DO

Because you're human, you're going to generate some negativity. Don't despair. Like a baby, you learn to walk by falling down and getting up again and again. Eventually, you fall less often, learn to walk, climb stairs, maybe even run a marathon. Avoiding negativity takes effort and vigilance. If you do 'fall by the wayside', you can purify your negativity and start afresh with a clean slate by taking the following steps:

- Own up to what you have done and who you have harmed. Meditate on the benefits of practising positive acts that are motivated by love and compassion.
- Do something positive to counteract your negativity. This can be anything from saying prayers to specifically helping the person you've harmed.
- Generate sincere regret by contemplating the hurt you've caused.
- Resolve to refrain from this negative action in the future.

In order for an act to have fully negative consequences, it must have four components. First, someone or something has to be at the receiving end of the harmful action. Second, the intention behind the act must be to do harm. Third, you have to actually commit the act. Fourth, you relish the fact that you have done so. If any or some of the four do not apply, the negative consequences for you will be reduced.

YOUR GUIDE TO LIVING AN ETHICAL LIFE

Besides avoiding negative actions, the Buddha recommended three effective ways to increase your positive karma and live a happy and fulfilled life. As you work with these guidelines, you'll experience how profoundly transformative they can be. The traditional teachings liken them to moonlight and a cool breeze on a summer night. Practising them cools the heat of your delusions and negativity.

HONOUR YOUR COMMITMENTS

In order to live and work in harmony with others, you make promises and agreements. When you take a job, for example, you commit to exchange your labour for a paycheque. You enter into business relationships with a contract, a handshake or verbal agreement, thereby promising to perform a service or provide material goods. When you sign a lease, you agree to take care of a property and pay the rent on time.

You also make less formal commitments on a daily basis: you promise to take your child to the zoo; you commit to cleaning out the garage or performing other household tasks; you vow to yourself that you will not overspend your budget.

You enter into a more long-term commitment when you take a marriage vow to love and cherish your partner. In certain religious traditions, you may take vows to refrain from harmful practices and live in accordance with the teachings you've been given.

When you don't keep your commitments, you undermine your relationships with others, with your higher power and with yourself. You also cause harm that will have karmic consequences over time. Try to honour all your vows and commitments, even those that seem small and insignificant. Doing so

JOURNAL EXERCISE

Spend some time writing about the vows and commitments you currently have. Ask yourself if you've been honouring them as best you can. What could you do to be more reliable and conscientious as a marriage partner, a business associate, a parent or a friend? If you have committed to take better care of the environment, what are you doing to fulfil your promise? If you've taken religious vows, ask yourself if you are keeping them pure and intact.

will make your life less stressful because you will create congruence between what you say and what you do.

WORK ON YOUR SPIRITUAL GROWTH

Spiritual growth does not mean becoming 'holy'. It means embracing your life and becoming a more caring, loving, compassionate person. It means, as the old song goes, 'accentuating the positive and eliminating the negative'. Be

vigilant and fight your delusions of attachment, anger and ignorance. Work against any negative habitual patterns. Purify any wrongdoing and let it go. Try not to let your past negativity prevent you from embracing a more positive life. Be happy about any spiritual growth you've experienced thus far. Read something that inspires you every day and meditate on what you've read. Be willing to explore the deeper truths about yourself and your existence. Seek out the company of others who are also interested in spiritual growth, and avoid those who try to turn you away from your spiritual path.

If you find you need professional help to work through your problems, don't hesitate to get therapy or counselling. Work on your spiritual growth by becoming the best person you can be.

LET GO OF GUILT MEDITATION

Find a time and place where you can be alone and undisturbed, then contemplate the following:

Sincere regret has the power to reduce my delusions and negative behaviour because it will inspire me to change. Guilt will not help me. It will make me feel hopelessly stuck in shame and unworthiness, and unable to take positive action to improve my life, either in the present or in the future. Everything is impermanent, including my negative actions. If I sincerely own up to what I have done, regret any harm I have caused, do something to make up for it and promise never to repeat the action, I can release any shame I feel for having caused harm. I can free my energy to overcome my problems and work diligently to be a better person.

HELP OTHERS

The Buddha's third recommendation is one you'll be familiar with from the first key, Let it go. You can also practise generosity in Do no harm, and the Buddha suggests even more ways you can be of service (see pages 48–49).

By focusing on the needs of others, you not only avoid negative activities, but also the disturbing emotions at their root. You cut down on selfishness, self-absorption, self-cherishing, and shut the door on the negativity that brings you misery and unhappiness.

The Buddha suggested that you regard the needs of others as important, or more important than your own. It's a tall order in a society that encourages us to consider ourselves as the centre of the universe.

It can seem like a lot to ask to spend your precious time helping others, but you'll find it lifts your spirits and makes your days more enjoyable and rewarding. Besides, if you're busy focusing on the needs of others, you'll have less time to cause harm.

THE BUDDHA'S 11 GREAT WAYS TO HELP OTHERS

1 Support your family, relatives and friends by creating wealth through ethical business practice.

2 Befriend people who are confused. Help friends or family members with drinking or drug problems to get the support they need. Volunteer to help troubled teenagers.

3 Welcome strangers, give them shelter and provide for their other needs. Immigrants and people fleeing repressive governments need support to make a new start. Volunteer to help them through churches or not-for-profit organizations.

4 Protect people who are living in fear. Work for a battered women's shelter, for instance, or help people displaced by floods, storms and other natural disasters.

5 Help those grieving over loss or separation. Grieving takes time. Commit to helping a friend or loved one get back on his or her feet after losing someone through death or divorce, no matter how long it takes.

6 Give material and spiritual support. Be as generous as you can with your knowledge, time, money and possessions.

7 Help people with their positive aspirations. If you know someone who is positively motivated to study for a qualification, start a business, study music or world religions, support them in any way you can.

8 Help people overcome obstacles to their wellbeing. Illness, debt and redundancy can be devastating. Try to be there for people when they face serious problems.

9 Support those who are trying to live an ethical life. Help friends and family members who are struggling to avoid situations that trigger their negativity. If you invite a recovering alcoholic to a dinner party, don't serve alcohol.

10 Help people who are engaged in destructive activities by refusing to condone their negative behaviour. If you know a friend who is stealing or is involved in shady business practices, you can help by confronting them with the truth of their actions.

11 Help by using any special gifts you may have. Whatever skills or talents you possess, share them freely with the motivation to be helpful to others.

KEY 3

BITE YOUR TONGUE

The third of the Buddha's keys deals with anger. This key is traditionally known as 'Patience', but not the kind of patience that enables you to wait hours for your new lover to arrive for dinner. Rather, it's practising patience as an antidote to anger. It's biting your tongue instead of getting angry when someone harms you. It means being unflappable in the face of suffering or difficulty. It also means having the patience to stick to your spiritual path.

Anger may seem like a source of power and a way to protect yourself, but it's you who suffers most when you get angry. Your blood pressure shoots up and, for that moment, you are consumed with your story of whatever it is that has made you angry. It is as though you are hijacked by your own emotions, and your heart contracts and takes on armour — the opposite of what you want it

to do. Real power comes from a calm and centred place. You can learn to set boundaries and protect yourself without closing down your heart and your connection to others.

The Buddha's main message is to help others and avoid harm. If you strike back with anger when someone hurts you, you have a problem, because you are harming others. It's also impossible to help people when you're in that state of mind. If you choose to get angry, you won't be able to make positive use of the inevitable suffering and hardship life presents. You won't be able to use these difficult situations

to grow — emotionally or spiritually. If you don't have the patience to study and practise a spiritual path, you won't become a better, happier person.

If you've stayed with the book this far, you will have learned how to generate positive karma by living the Buddha's first two keys. With Let it go, you learned the joys and benefits of generosity, and with Do no harm, you learned how to increase your happiness by living an ethical life. The Buddha also taught that you can destroy all the positive energy you've generated with just one big temper tantrum. That's how powerful and negative anger can be.

Isn't anger justified when someone harms you? The Buddha argued that it never is. You may feel it's reasonable to be angry and frustrated when you have a serious illness or a drunken driver ploughs into your car. Again the

Buddha is insistent: getting angry always hurts you and never helps. Isn't it important to feel anger to counteract injustice? He's clear on this point, too: the only remedy for injustice is action motivated by compassion.

Because the Buddha wanted to emphasize the importance of patience, he described it as the finest jewellery you could wear — think of it as the diamond necklace of the keys. He also likened patience to armour because it protects you from negativity. And

because anger can make you physically unattractive, he called it the best beauty cream available. He recommended patience as the best way to relieve unhappiness — your own and other people's. When you completely transform your anger, you achieve what he called 'mirror-like wisdom'. This wisdom gives you the ability to lovingly and uncritically take in and reflect back

THINGS TO DO

Start working with your anger by consciously intervening when it arises. Begin with someone who simply irritates you — perhaps a telemarketer who calls during dinner. When you answer the call and feel your irritation rise, stop. Focus on the person on the other end of the line and consider the following: Just like you, he or she wants to be

happy and is simply trying to pay their bills. Just like you, this person is trying to avoid suffering. Consider all the ways you may be alike. Do they have kids, or a dog? Do they sound stressed? As you return your focus to what the person is saying, even if they are being aggressive, try to be polite and get off the phone gracefully.

Now, consider how you feel. Breathe in any remaining irritation and let it open your heart. Breathe out kindness towards the person on the phone and every other telemarketer working to make ends meet. If your anger got the best of you, don't despair. Hang up and, when you can, think about the person in the way described above. How do these thoughts affect your mood? How does your body feel?

whatever life presents you, while remaining calm and unchanged. In other words, you are no longer vulnerable to the pain or destructive consequences of your anger – for yourself or others. The Buddha's viewpoints may seem counter-intuitive to you — even radical — but, as you'll see, he offered some compelling arguments to make his case.

JOURNAL EXERCISE

You may have feelings of anger that you can't explain. If so, get out your journal. Divide your page into two columns and have a conversation with yourself. In the left column write as if you are your own parent, and ask yourself what you are feeling. In the right column, respond as the child within you, without censoring or editing what you write. You're already angry so, rather than try to suppress your emotions, it will help to find out their root cause. You may discover that, beneath your anger, you are feeling afraid, sad or lonely. If this is the case, try to take some positive steps to address your needs.

If your anger persists, identify the source. If you're angry with a person, meditate on the reasons why anger is harmful. If you're angry as a result of a financial or health problem, try to embrace the situation rather than remain in opposition to it, and work to resolve it.

HOW TO HAVE PATIENCE WHEN SOMEONE HARMS YOU

The first form of patience enables you to refrain from anger when somebody harms you. That person could be someone you've harmed in the past, someone you've never harmed, or even someone you're close to and to whom you've shown great kindness — the last is often the most difficult to deal with.

Refraining from anger may at times seem like an unfair, impossible or even ridiculous request. If someone steals your credit card, you may reason that anger is a perfectly justifiable response. But take a closer look at this situation. Perhaps the person stealing from you is doing you a favour. If the

thief had not acted in this way to harm you, you wouldn't be able to practise patience and work towards enlightenment. Instead of anger, the Buddha suggested your first response could actually be gratitude.

You might also consider that the people who harm you are victims of their own delusions. These delusions were present in their former lives and have taken root in their present ones. Because they haven't learned to work with their attachment, anger or ignorance, they're in the grip of these powerful negative emotions. So instead of getting angry, try to feel compassion. Not only is the person who has harmed you unhappy, they are also generating yet more bad karma for themselves.

Which brings us to the following point. If you choose to retaliate with anger, you're only causing yourself more suffering in the future. The negative karma you generate for yourself will eventually have consequences. In other words, directing your anger at the person who relieved you of your credit card, wishing them harm, hoping they'll suffer because of what they did to you, will accomplish nothing and hurt you in the end. The reason you became a victim of the credit card thief was because you generated negative karma in the past. Who knows, it could be that in a former life you yourself were a thief.

But karma is not a guilt and blame game. It's more like a law of nature: what goes around comes around. The biblical version is 'what you sow, you reap'. Essentially, karma teaches that it's better to protect yourself and manage your own behaviour than point fingers and seek revenge.

When the Buddha asked you to refrain from anger, was he suggesting you be a doormat? Was he asking you to make yourself vulnerable to abuse? The answer is an emphatic 'No!' It's important that you retain healthy boundaries. You have a right and also an obligation to protect yourself from physical or financial harm. If you *are* harmed, you have a right to seek redress and compensation. But you can do this without being angry.

Finally, by purifying your own negative karma, the Buddha taught that you will cut down on the harm caused to you by others. In this way, you can avoid or at least mitigate the consequences of your past, negative actions.

CHERISHING THOSE WHO ARE DIFFICULT MEDITATION

If I simply read about the Buddha's keys and I don't have any opportunity to practise them, what good will that do me? Every opportunity I have to work with my anger is a gift. Because I would like to one day achieve ultimate happiness for myself and help others do the same, I need to reduce and eventually eliminate my anger. When someone difficult enters my life and 'pushes my buttons', I will cherish their presence, because that person is giving me a chance to work on my anger. I will try to get beyond my irritation or even rage, by focusing on our common humanity – our mutual desire to find happiness and avoid suffering.

VISUALIZATION

Imagine you're having a special holiday meal with your family. One of your relatives starts criticizing you. The more he or she has to drink, the worse it gets. This person can't seem to leave you alone, and it's not the first time you've had to endure the onslaught. As usual, you feel your anger starting to rise but, instead of lashing out, you remember to Bite your tongue. You remind yourself that he or she is drunk and being held hostage by his or her anger.

At the moment you let go of your anger, notice your relative's harsh words transform into tiny arrows that fall harmlessly on the table between you. As the arrows hit the tablecloth, they become beautiful flowers. Visualize yourself picking them up, fashioning them into a flower garland and offering it to your relative. For years you thought of this person as insufferable, but now you see them as they are — a human being who is suffering, just like you. Your usual, angry response is transformed into compassion.

HOW TO HAVE PATIENCE WHEN LIFE GETS DIFFICULT

Because you're human, you encounter difficulties — which is when you need to draw on the Buddha's second kind of patience. The problem may be mundane, such as a washing machine leaking all over the kitchen floor and down through the ceiling below. Or you may come up against something serious, such as losing your job unexpectedly, or being told by your doctor that you have cancer. The list of what can go wrong in life is endless. You can resolve one problem one day, only to have a new one spring up in the next. The question is not whether you'll have challenges and difficulties — you have and will. The question is how you will cope and respond to them.

When life gives you a black eye, your first response may be denial. If your heating stops working in the dead of winter, you ask yourself how it could possibly be true. When you take in the reality and realize that your boiler

needs to be replaced, your next response may be anger. You may look for someone to blame — the person who sold you the house, the repairman who didn't warn you this might happen, the boiler manufacturer or your spouse, who should have known to put money away for this kind of emergency. You may just feel angry that it happened to *you*, regardless of who's responsible.

But experiencing life as a personal affront and entertaining denial and anger are, at the very least, ineffective tactics. These mental states drain your energy and vitality when you need them most and burden those around you who are trying to cope. Accepting suffering and not taking it personally will actually lessen your mental and physical pain. By facing suffering, you'll inspire yourself to be free of it for good. Eliminate all your negativity, create virtue, recognize wisdom, generate love and compassion, and you'll eventually become enlightened. This is the Buddhist way, although it can work within other spiritual traditions as well. If you run from suffering and difficulties, you won't develop yourself spiritually. The days and weeks will go by and soon become years. Living in denial of your misery, you won't be motivated to do anything about it.

Your patience in the face of your suffering becomes your armour. It protects you from the negativity of other people and the slings and arrows of life. The more you face and accept your suffering, the more you can bear. You grow in your capacity to take on your own suffering and the suffering of others.

THINGS TO DO

If you drive, you are bound to come across rude or angry behaviour. The next time another driver cuts in front of you and nearly causes an accident or refuses to let you into lane when you need to get off at the next exit, *rejoice*, because you've just been given an excellent

opportunity to work on your patience. Instead of shouting, 'I can't believe what he just did!', swearing or retaliating by doing something equally dangerous, Bite your tongue. Take a few deep breaths and stay focused on the road ahead. Accept what has

happened, generate compassion for the person driving so carelessly, and wish for them relief from their anger and suffering.

We admire the men and women in films, novels or in real life who are calm and cool in the face of adversity, who accept the situation and deal with it. You may feel inspired and uplifted to witness their strength. You may admire their effective, intelligent and constructive response to challenges and tragedies. You'll notice they don't have time for denial, anger, resistance or complaints. They are presented with life's difficulties and work their way through them. The rescue workers who worked at the scene of the World Trade Center in New York are a wonderful example of real-life heroes. They demonstrated great courage, compassion and selflessness. As firefighters, police and emergency workers, they had already developed an ability to bear suffering. They are willing to bear suffering because serving others gives their life higher meaning and purpose. Why not strive to emulate them and become a spiritual warrior yourself?

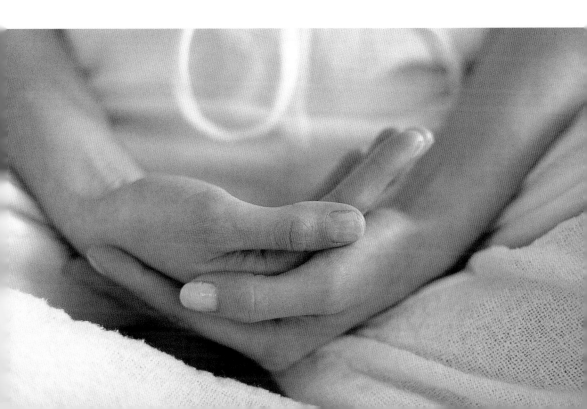

I WILL ACCEPT WHAT HAPPENS TODAY MEDITATION

When you wake up in the morning, contemplate the following:

I will be fully present and accepting of all life brings me this day.

Whatever joys or sorrows I encounter, I will greet them with patience and equanimity.

If today brings difficulties, I will accept them wholeheartedly and work to resolve them to the best of my ability.

I vow not to let anger or resentment cloud my vision or judgment.

I will strive to increase my capacity to bear my own difficulties so that I can develop my love and compassion for others.

HOW TO HAVE PATIENCE ON YOUR SPIRITUAL PATH

You'll need the third type of patience to give you the courage and dedication to stay on your spiritual path, whatever that may be. This route that you take to try to reduce your negative thinking and activity and build your positive virtue is never easy or steady. You'll have good days and bad. You need the patience to work on yourself over the long haul, or it will be hard to realize the rewards promised by the Buddha, Christ, Yahweh, Mohammed and the other great spiritual masters. Frustration is part of the path and patience will get your through.

For most people, a spiritual life is last on the list, after work, going out, hanging out with friends or shopping. Practising patience on your spiritual path means making your spiritual development a priority. It means working to understand spiritual truths, and not letting yourself be distracted from your mission to make yourself the happiest person you can be. Your spiritual growth will be supported by some sort of daily practice. Learning, reading, meditating, praying, writing in a journal, attending group services — all of these will help build the right muscles.

THINGS TO DO

Irrational thinking can keep you locked in anger. The following thought patterns all undermine your ability to develop patience:

- **Exaggeration.** Watch your tendency to over-generalize — for example, 'He *always* avoids responsibility'. Try not to think in terms of 'always', 'never' or 'should'.

- **Making assumptions.** Try not to jump to conclusions when you don't know the facts. If someone is late for an appointment and you feel your anger rising, think of several reasons why they might not have arrived rather than assume they're just being irresponsible.

- **Black-and-white thinking.** Thinking in terms of right and wrong, good or bad and either/or can easily lead to anger. Make efforts to understand and accept other people rather than judge them.

- **Emotion-based reasoning.** An example of this is when you believe someone has actually rejected you, because that's the way you *feel* — which then justifies your anger. Stop yourself whenever you automatically equate your feelings with reality.

If you've never been shown how to meditate, start practising by just sitting and watching your breath for ten minutes a day (see Key 5). It will strengthen your mind's ability to focus and concentrate on the keys and other spiritual teachings of your choice.

SOUNDS GOOD BUT WHAT'S IN IT FOR ME?

The Buddha worked hard to make his case for practising patience. Here are some additional reasons he gave to convince you to practise Biting your tongue:

- You'll have fewer enemies. It's inevitable that some people you encounter in life will dislike you and try to hurt you. If you practise patience, you'll dramatically decrease the number of people who wish you harm.

- You'll keep your friends. If your past is littered with burned bridges and relationships gone sour, anger may be the culprit.

- It will bring you peace and joy. In these stressful times, we need all the peace and joy we can get.

- If you have less anger, you'll have less regret. How often have you felt remorse after lashing out at someone? How wonderful it would be not to feel that.

- You'll die in peace. On a karmic level, the worst thing you can do for yourself is die an angry person.

WHAT HAPPENS IF I DON'T PRACTISE PATIENCE?

It's clear that having patience brings you a lot of advantages. Now let's look at the flipside, or what happens when you *don't* practise patience.

- Anger destroys all the good karma you've created. It makes 'toast' out of

your hard-won virtues. Who needs this when it's so hard to practise virtue and accumulate good karma?

- If you're angry you don't have peace of mind. You destroy all feelings of joy and serenity.
- Chronic anger will disrupt your sleep and destroy your health.
- Anger is stressful. If your mind is agitated, you won't be able to think or function well in your daily life.
- Anger makes you forget all the kindness people have shown you. It distorts your view of them and means that you disregard their good qualities and actions.
- If you're an angry person, you'll lose your friends. They'll eventually tire of your negativity and move on.

ANGER MANAGEMENT BUDDHIST-STYLE

According to the Buddha, you've been angry for lifetimes so reducing your anger is bound to take both practice and patience. One of the best ways to develop your patience is to read about it, think about it and meditate on it. Unless you make these ideas a part of your thinking, the next time your Aunt Helen tells you, for the hundredth time, how you should lose weight, you will probably blow up at her. To override an habitual tendency to get angry, you need to make the Buddha's ideas resonate on a feeling level.

Tibetan Buddhists call this type of meditation 'analytical meditation'. When you practise it, you read and study, then you put down your book or papers and think about what you've read. You try to put the material into your own words and apply it to situations in your own life. When you begin to feel an emotional resonance with what you've studied — a kind of heartfelt understanding — you try to stay with that feeling as long as you can. You end your meditation with a prayer, asking that you be able to put what you've learned into practice when the need arises.

Analytical meditation works by changing your mind. Try to think and meditate on a daily basis about anger: its negative influence on your life and its consequences in future lives. Write about your insights in your journal. Slowly, and over time, you'll find your anger lessening. This is how Buddhists manage their anger.

THINGS TO DO

If you're angry with a friend, colleague, your spouse or boss, remove yourself from their company. If that's not possible, ask if you can talk at another time. Instead of dwelling on how you were wronged, review the material in this chapter. Meditate for a few minutes on any points that help. Before you go to bed, think about all the positive qualities of that person. Then get a good night's sleep. If your anger has subsided by the morning, make contact and try to heal the rift.

KEY 4

SWEAT IT OUT

The fourth key, Sweat it out, means being enthusiastic about achieving enlightenment. To return to the original meaning of the word enthusiasm, it's the notion of 'having God within'. Ultimate happiness or enlightenment is not just for the chosen few. All beings have the potential to become enlightened, from the lowly ant to Mother Teresa. If you persevere with enthusiasm, you'll make it eventually. Achievement is one per cent inspiration and 99 per cent perspiration, so the old saying goes, and the Buddha wholeheartedly agreed.

DEVELOP YOUR POTENTIAL

Developing your potential and becoming a happier and more helpful person sounds great on paper, but you may think that you have so many problems and difficulties, you can't possibly hope to overcome them. You're too old, too mean, too deluded, too angry and too jealous, so why should you bother? If you have this kind of mindset, it can be tempting to give up before you begin. Perhaps, unconsciously, you don't feel worthy of achieving enlightenment. Or perhaps you doubt that it is possible to be free from all negativity and suffering.

The Buddha was just like you and he achieved enlightenment. He had belief in every being's ability to do what he did, and a great desire to relieve your suffering. That's why he bothered to share the keys and his other

teachings. If and when you feel disheartened, he recommended meditating on what he called your 'precious human life', and all the opportunities that this life affords.

The truth is that no one has ever achieved anything without enthusiasm and perseverance. It's an essential ingredient in any endeavour, and a key on which the other five keys depend. The opposite of enthusiasm is laziness, which has never brought about achievement of any kind. If you have enthusiasm for working with the keys, not only will you move yourself closer to enlightenment, you'll also bring energy to everything you do.

WISH-FULFILLING JEWEL MEDITATION

My life is a wish-fulfilling jewel. With it, I have the potential to achieve ultimate happiness and enlightenment and be of great help to others. Amazingly, I have life in which I can access not only the Buddha's teachings, but also all the spiritual teachings I could ever want, and the opportunity to pursue them. Tibetan Buddhists would say my life is as rare as if a blind turtle

came to the surface of the ocean once every hundred years and somehow managed to put her head through a single golden yoke floating on the water. What are the chances of that happening? Here I am, alive and full of potential. I have a good mind and the desire to be a better person. I can either use my time wisely or waste my life in countless ways.

THE THREE KINDS OF ENTHUSIASM

The Buddha taught three types of enthusiasm. All three are essential to your work on the keys. They each build on the others and give you the fuel to achieve lasting happiness.

BE DETERMINED TO GET FREE

The first type of enthusiasm is so important it is also one of the three main principles of the Buddhist path. It rests on the First Noble Truth that 'all in life is suffering'. Although it may sound negative at first, it's an important concept to grasp if you want to achieve true happiness.

You need to appreciate that underneath your happiest moments lies suffering in order to be able to recognize the myriad ways you are drawn into mistaking temporary happiness for ultimate happiness. Without the determination to be free from these sufferings, you won't have any desire to make use of the keys or any other spiritual path. This may sound wrong to you. How could your happiness actually be suffering? Before you leap to judgment, let's consider this idea more deeply.

For instance, when you fall madly, deliriously in love, you feel ecstatically happy — yet when you separate you feel tremendous pain. That's attachment at work. When you buy a new car, you're excited and happy, but the happiness is tarnished because the car immediately starts to deteriorate and depreciate.

That's the reality behind 'all life is change'. If you examine your life closely, you'll notice that ordinary happiness doesn't last; desire eventually leads to unhappiness; and deluded thinking and anger always deliver negative consequences. If you pay attention, you'll begin to notice that your habitual ways of dealing with the world — anger and attachment — provide temporary relief but don't deliver the permanent happiness you're seeking.

So, in practising this first form of enthusiasm, you decide not to settle for fleeting moments of pleasure, but 'go for the gold' and seek out ultimate happiness for yourself and everyone else on the planet. You need a big heart because you're making a serious commitment. You're deciding to become enlightened to benefit yourself and all living beings. It's as though you've pledged to train for the spiritual version of the Olympics. Don't worry if you've never darkened the door of a church or even had a spiritual thought. The Buddha guarantees that, with enough determination and perseverance, you too can become a completely happy human being, free from suffering and negativity, and full of love and compassion for all beings.

Let's not pretend it's easy to develop this first enthusiasm. Life's attractions and addictions are so tantalizing. It's hard to let go of the belief that possessions, power, fame, food, alcohol, drugs, money, sex, marriage or children will make you ultimately happy. It's only when you spend some time thinking about all of these that you realize they can never completely deliver. When you come to this realization, it will be easier for you to find the determination to be free.

Does this mean you can't enjoy life? Absolutely not! When you have the determination to be free, you'll enjoy life on a deeper level, because you will be free of unrealistic expectation. You can enjoy the sensuous pleasures of life fully because you understand they are fleeting. That strawberry will be even more delicious than before and your lovemaking will be that much more satisfying, because you won't pin your total happiness on it. You'll be able to love more deeply and have more compassion, without the strings of attachment. You will become a happier person because you have set yourself on a course that produces real happiness. And you don't have to wait until

VISUALIZATION

I have taken on a commitment to achieve enlightenment for the benefit of all living beings, including myself. I am practising the keys in order to move myself toward that ultimate happiness. I have a big heart: the heart of a warrior and hero. I have a tender heart and am sensitive to the suffering of all beings. I am willing to do what it takes to deliver myself and everyone else from suffering. With my enthusiasm and determination to get free, I feel like Joan of Arc or Sir Lancelot, dressed in jewel-encrusted armour. I'm no longer pulled away from my mission by the countless distractions that used to consume my life. I now have meaning and direction. I won't let myself or anyone else down because I have a clear focus and the will to succeed.

you become enlightened. When you begin to work with the keys, you begin to experience the joy of generosity, the grounding that comes with having a moral compass, the serenity that comes from practising patience, and the enthusiasm and perseverance to achieve your goal of true happiness. You will be more joyful because you are actively seeking to develop your love and compassion for yourself and others. When you have the determination to be free, life gets so much better.

THINGS TO DO

When you begin to generate enthusiasm for your spiritual development, your enthusiasm for work, relationships and other activities will also increase. Enthusiasm helps you set priorities, focus and energize yourself to complete any task — from preparing dinner, to writing a novel, to becoming enlightened. By being enthusiastic and willing to persevere, you add the elements of joy and love to whatever you do.

At work, your enthusiasm will not only help you, it will also help energize and inspire your fellow workers and team members. In your relationships, your enthusiasm and willingness to engage with your partner, relatives, friends and children will strengthen your love and the bonds of affection.

Your ability to be patient and persevere through hardships will sustain and deepen your relationships.

DEVELOP ENTHUSIASTIC COMMITMENT

Once you have resolved to become enlightened, the second enthusiasm — to commit to practising the keys — follows naturally. Instead of clinging to your habitual negative patterns, you will find that you are eager to let them go. You will want to build up your positive qualities because you understand how this can deliver the happiness you seek. You will practise generosity, monitor your anger, strive to develop patience, work diligently to avoid harming yourself and others, and nurture your enthusiasm and perseverance. As your enthusiasm grows, you will become interested in meditating on the keys and making them a part of your life. You will begin to think about them on a daily basis and write about them in your journal. If you practise another tradition, you will become more interested in and diligent about practising that path as well. Possessing enthusiastic commitment increases your happiness on a daily basis.

HELP OTHERS

The third enthusiasm is a part of every key, which shows its importance. As you become happier and more content, you will naturally want to help others experience the same. Should you go door-to-door early on a Saturday morning armed with pamphlets on the keys? The Buddha wasn't big on proselytizing. He preferred the attraction method. If people notice you are less angry, more loving and upbeat, they may ask how you got to be that way. If they're interested, share what you know without instructing them. The Buddha preferred that you work on yourself, and help others using any of the ways mentioned in the previous keys. With your enthusiasm on board, helping others will be easier and more enjoyable.

WHAT'S YOUR STYLE OF LAZINESS?

The opposite of sweating it out is laziness. You may understand laziness as a kind of lethargy. In fact, it may be another form of laziness that is undermining your path to happiness. Laziness can mean becoming discouraged, procrastinating, whiling away your time in trivial pursuits or being incredibly busy. What's your style?

'I JUST CAN'T DO IT'

We touched upon this form of opting out in the introduction to this chapter, but it bears repeating. This is the laziness of discouragement. If you are lazy in this way, you believe the whole enlightenment thing is beyond you. You think, 'How could someone like me gain all the qualities of the Buddha?' You think this way because the idea of developing yourself is unsettling. You're afraid of even trying. But think about it: you have nowhere to go but up. You have nothing to lose and everything to gain.

The Buddha said that he was in pretty bad shape until he worked on himself and achieved enlightenment. He emphasized that *anyone*, however weak, angry, jealous or generally lost can achieve enlightenment. Why put it off for eons, when you can take control of your destiny and have ultimate happiness in this lifetime?

'I WAS BORN WITH A PROCRASTINATION GENE'

Procrastination will certainly be an obstacle on your spiritual path. But, sorry, you can't blame your DNA. It really is just a bad habit, and one you can overcome with a little effort.

First, consider how you feel when you put things off for another day. You may experience momentary relief, but underneath you know you're cheating yourself out of the deep satisfaction of giving your all. Whether it's deferment on a mundane level, or a way to avoid working toward achieving enlightenment, procrastination will create suffering and keep you from happiness. Meditating on these points will spur you to action when the desire to put things off rears its ugly head. You'll learn to recognize when that lazy response is coming on, and intervene by taking just one positive step forward. You don't have to do everything at once: just take one manageable step at a time. When working Bite your tongue, for example, commit to curtailing an angry response just once a day and build from there.

'I LOVE PLAYING TRIVIAL PURSUIT'

It's easy to fill your life with endless entertainment, romantic quests, surfing the Internet, escapist reading and other distractions. It's not that these activities are wrong in themselves, but if they take over your life, you clearly have a problem with priorities. You may be cheating yourself by not making the best use of your time. As a way to combat this form of laziness, remind yourself that you have a precious human life, that everything is impermanent, and life is relatively short. Let these thoughts kick-start your enthusiasm for working with the keys.

BUBBLE MEDITATION

The world and all its inhabitants are impermanent. My life is rare and precious and also fragile, like a bubble in water that forms quickly then disappears. It's uncertain when I will die. Simply taking advantage of the opportunity to reduce my suffering in this life makes my efforts at spiritual development worthwhile. If I reduce my anger and miserliness, for example, not only will I be helping others around me, but I will also feel happier. On the other hand, if I spend all my time in a fantasyland of escapist distractions, I will not be able to consciously address my problems.

Because of my growing sense of compassion toward myself and others, I'm inspired to make better choices about my use of time. If I don't utilize the short time I have, I will have lost an opportunity to achieve enlightenment, or at the very least to ensure my future life is a good one. I need to grab this opportunity while I can, to secure my own and the happiness of others. I can start now and use the time I have left to full advantage. I will do that by generating enthusiasm for overcoming my negativity and generating positive qualities. Every day I will express gratitude that I'm alive and have this fantastic opportunity to work toward experiencing the bliss of enlightenment, for my benefit and the benefit of all other beings.

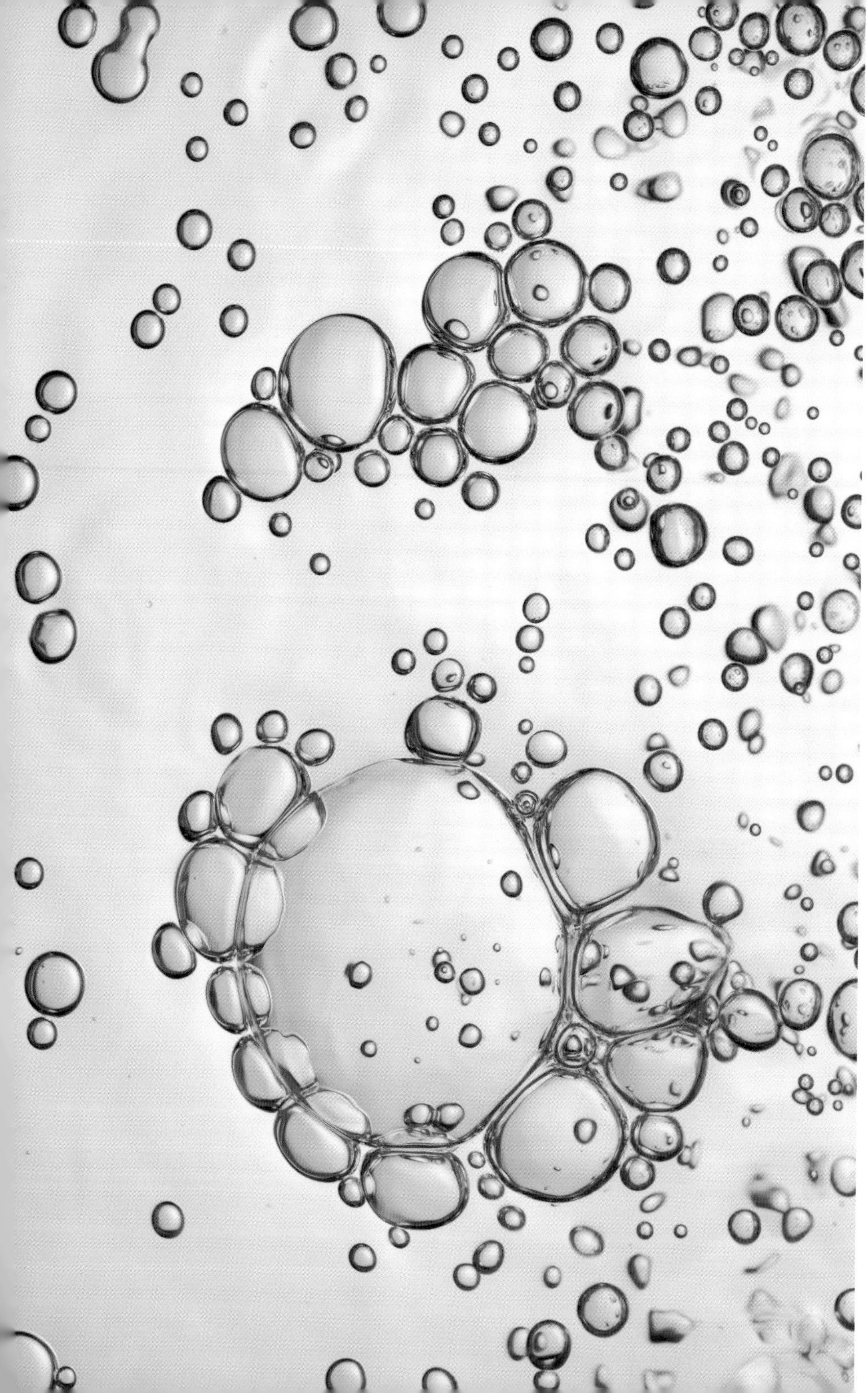

'I'M SO BUSY'

Being incredibly busy is one way to ensure you don't have time to work with the keys. Having an over-booked appointment calendar may make you feel dynamic and important, but frenetic activity doesn't accomplish anything toward your ultimate happiness. Ask yourself what you are avoiding by staying busy. Take a hard look at your schedule and make time for helping yourself and others.

JOURNAL EXERCISE

Keep track of all your activities for a week by writing them in your journal. Try to be as thorough as possible. At the end of the week, review what you've done. What supported and what detracted you from practising the keys? What activities undermined your enthusiasm?

When you analyze how you use your time, you may discover some interesting patterns and habits. For instance, you may find you spend much more time than you thought surfing the Internet or answering and reading email. You may find you watch much more television than you thought you did, or shop more than you really need. Consider how you can rearrange your schedule or eliminate activities to make it easier to meditate, read about and work with the keys. Try to create a schedule that shifts your priorities to more positive and beneficial activities. Test it out over the next week and see if your enthusiasm gets a boost.

JOURNAL EXERCISE

Gehlek Rimpoche, a Tibetan Buddhist lama, has lived and taught in the
United States for over 15 years. He's had a lot of time to observe the
types of laziness that manifest in a modern society. He says that having
grown up in old Tibet, his version of laziness was sitting under a tree
and taking a nap. But what he has observed since moving to America
is what he calls 'busy lazy'. In other words, he sees a lot of people
running around, going nowhere fast. Spiritual work is last on their list,
if it's on there at all.

Write a few pages in your journal about your form of laziness.
Maybe you're a throwback from older times, and when you feel the
urge to activity, you lie down until it
passes. More likely, you tend toward
'busy lazy' — it's hard not to be
affected by the constant stimulation
and speed of present-day life.
Whatever your style of laziness,
become conscious of how it
undermines your enthusiasm for
helping yourself and others. Look at
'Four ways to keep on keeping on'
(see page 83) for ways to build your
enthusiasm back up.

THINGS TO DO

The Buddha talked a lot about suffering but he was actually a fun-loving person. If he wasn't, he wouldn't have pushed bliss and happiness in such a big way. When you work with the keys yourself, try to make it as fun as possible. This will keep you enthusiastically involved and happy to get up in the morning. If you like entertainment, for example, don't give it up, just transform it into a positive activity. Go to the cinema, theatre and rock concerts with the idea of applying

the keys to all you hear or see. When you see a character being generous, notice how this makes you feel. When you see a character consumed by their anger and hatred, notice how they are harming themselves as well as everyone else. Listen to the lyrics of popular songs and identify the 'delusion *du jour*': perhaps someone swearing to get revenge on an old lover or someone raving about the joys of addiction. On the other hand, you may hear a song that moves you and inspires you to more love and compassion. Keep yourself interested and engaged in any creative way that works for you.

FOUR WAYS TO KEEP ON KEEPING ON

First, *aspire* to practising the keys. The definition of 'aspiration' is the will to succeed or a cherished desire to accomplish something. Make up your mind to achieve ultimate happiness by working with the keys. Recall that in Do no harm, the Buddha taught that we should help others with their aspirations. He knew how hard it is to achieve anything without first aspiring to do so.

Second, make your practice interesting and joyful. Make it fun. Bring your creativity to all that you do. If you like art, do an illustration of the keys; if you're a musician, write a song about your anger or desire. Your need to get to the point where all you want to do is develop yourself, like a child so engrossed in play you don't hear your parents calling you to dinner. You can only develop that much enthusiasm if you're having a good time.

Third, keep your enthusiasm flowing. Enthusiasm can be like a balloon — it can be blown up quickly, then suddenly deflate. Or it can be like a huge rainstorm followed by months of severe drought. You may become excited about the keys this week, only to forget about them in the next. Real enthusiasm requires steadfast perseverance and constancy over time. To keep on track, congratulate yourself on your self-reliance in working toward your enlightenment. Have confidence and belief in your ability to help others. Have faith in your ability to face down your delusions or disturbing emotions. Believe in your inner warrior.

The fourth way to keep on, if you get overwhelmed by working with the keys, is to take a break. An ability to relax and rejuvenate is essential to keeping your enthusiasm strong. If you are helping to take care of a sick friend, for instance, don't wear yourself out to the point where you get burned out. Know your limits and honour your need to rest.

THINGS TO DO

Rest and relaxation are essential when you work with the keys or you risk becoming emotionally unbalanced and physically exhausted. Balance is everything. Have the wisdom to know when to push, when to stop and how to regulate your energy. If you're meditating on the keys and you find yourself unable to concentrate, stop. Go for a walk, have a snack, take a nap. You may need to let it go for a day. If you're helping a sick relative, learn to recognize when you need a break. You're not going to be useful to others if you're irritable, stressed out and not taking care of your own needs. Resist any temptation to measure your enthusiasm against anyone else's. Your enthusiasm is unique to you and your path.

Consciously try new ways to relax and rejuvenate. Get a massage, take hot baths, stretch out for ten minutes and relax all your muscles

in turn. Learn to monitor your stress levels and recognize when stress and tension are working against you.

THE BENEFITS OF ENTHUSIASM

All achievement is rooted in enthusiasm. If you apply enthusiasm to your endeavours, you're bound to accomplish what you set out to do. Enthusiasm brings you both peace and pleasure. It's not only a stress reliever, it's also a source of fun. Enthusiasm helps you fulfil all your wishes. You won't get what you desire without it. Enthusiasm makes you pure. Enthusiasm for practising the Buddha's keys will reduce and eventually eliminate your negativity. Enthusiasm frees you from fear. You won't be afraid if you're happily engaged in helping yourself and others. Enthusiasm will deliver you to enlightenment. You can't get there from here without it.

SWEAT EQUITY

The most successful businesses in recent history started with little or no money. Amazon, Dell Computer, Microsoft, Apple and many wildly successful companies had their earliest beginning's in someone's bedroom or garage, where a small group of people worked extremely hard and invested their own 'sweat' to make their dreams come true. Bill Gates had to have enthusiasm for his ideas and belief in his ability to achieve success or Microsoft would not be what it is today. Jeff Bezos of Amazon left a lucrative job as an investment banker because he had a crazy idea that he could sell books online. In his enthusiasm, he wrapped Amazon's first book orders on his knees, on the floor of his garage. A family member suggested he try using a table.

Only you can achieve enlightenment. No outside investor can do it for you. You can't hire staff to work on your negative emotions or an accountant to keep a tally on your progress. You alone have to Sweat it out. Your sweat equity will appreciate rapidly and be well worth the effort.

THE DOWNSIDES OF LAZINESS

- If you don't have the enthusiasm to achieve ultimate happiness, you will have to wait a very long time — probably countless lifetimes — to achieve enlightenment.

- If you're preoccupied with the four kinds of laziness, chances are you won't have the time or energy to show generosity by giving of yourself or your possessions.

- As you've probably worked out by now, helping others is a major part of practising the keys. If you're lazy, you won't have a desire to help. Without enthusiasm, you undermine the principles of all the other keys and ultimately your whole practice.

THINGS TO DO

Whenever you feel discouraged, or feel like you're getting nowhere, think about everything you've accomplished — no matter how small or insignificant. If you've given a small gift to someone at work, rejoice in that. If you caught yourself before yelling at the kids, congratulate yourself. The Buddha would say you have had lifetimes to practise your negative habitual patterns so they're not going to evaporate overnight. Be happy you've finally started to loosen their grip on your life. Countless people never do. Feel happy you have found a method to help yourself. Concentrate on all you *have* done, rather than how far you have to go.

KEY 5

STICK TO THE POINT

The fifth key, Stick to the point, teaches you the important skills of focus and concentration. As you've already learned, working with the keys requires meditation as well as practice. You meditate on the keys by going over the points the Buddha made in relation to each one and applying them to your own life. As you meditate on the keys on a daily basis, they become more and more familiar and easier to practise. If you meditate on generosity, for example, you won't have to work so hard to be generous because the power of your meditation practice will help keep generosity in the forefront of your mind. Your anger will slowly lessen as you make the benefits of patience a part of your daily meditation. However, in order to meditate you need to have a stable, useful mind.

WHY LEARN TO CONCENTRATE?

If your mind is wandering, agitated or spaced-out when you sit down to think and meditate on the keys, you won't make much progress. Before you can practise analytical meditation — the kind of meditation we're talking about here, in which you think *about* something — you have to take a step back and learn how to focus and concentrate.

If you want to achieve success in any endeavour, worldly or otherwise, concentration is an absolute necessity. If you want to study, take exams or become a professional of any kind — athlete, doctor, nurse, business person,

scientist, concert musician, actor, carpenter, plumber or architect — you first have to be able to make use of your mind. If you can't, you won't be able to gain the knowledge you need to excel and perform well in your chosen field.

The keys are no exception. Without concentration, you won't be able to meditate and practise and, most importantly, you won't be able to understand their wisdom and become enlightened. This is why the fifth key is so very important. When you see images or statues of the Buddha, you almost always see him sitting in meditation. This is because he gained freedom from his own suffering by working with his mind. By focusing on positive thoughts, he eliminated the negative until he was able to grasp the true nature of reality and remove all negativity and suffering from his life. Happily, out of compassion, he decided to teach us how to do the same.

When your mind is focused on wholesome thoughts, you're avoiding negative ones. When your mind is unfocused and jumping here and there, it's easier to entertain the delusions — attachment, anger and ignorance — that get you into trouble and cause you unhappiness. You can end up thinking about all sorts of things when you are supposed to be meditating. For example, you may intend to think about generosity, but your mind jumps instead to what it would be like to have an affair with the new man or woman in the office, or wondering what's for dinner, or to an image of the car you want but can't afford, or how much you need a holiday. Pretty soon, you've completely forgotten what you set out to do: meditate on generosity. You might be sitting on a meditation cushion in London or Chicago, but your mind is driving an expensive car to a fancy restaurant in Hawaii with the new person at work.

On the other hand, when you have a focused and concentrated mind, you can gain tremendous control over your thought process. You have incredible mental power at your disposal to create a better life for yourself and others. Whatever you do becomes virtuous because you're avoiding negative thoughts.

THINGS TO DO

Prepare a nice meal at home and enjoy it, either by yourself or with family or friends. Then clear the table and ask everyone to retreat to another room. Fill your sink with warm, soapy water and begin washing the dishes. Pick up the first dish and start to scrub it clean. Try to focus and concentrate on the task in front of you and keep out extraneous

thoughts. Try to be mindful of every movement. Work slowly and deliberately. Stay fully present in the moment as if this is the most important thing you have ever done in your life. Notice the colour of the dishes, the beauty and functionality of your various kitchen tools and the sound of the water sloshing in the sink. If your mind strays, gently bring your focus back to the dishes in front of you.

Consider in what ways focusing and concentrating on this simple task changed it for you. Did washing the dishes become more interesting — even sensuous? Did you experience the power of being able to focus your mind fully in the present moment?

In order to help you focus and concentrate, the Buddha taught a kind of meditation knows as 'concentration meditation'. In this form of meditation you learn to calm and stabilize your mind.

WHAT IS CONCENTRATION MEDITATION?

Concentration meditation teaches you to concentrate your whole mind on
one object. The object can be your breath, a candle flame or an image such as
a picture of the Buddha, Christ or Mary. The only requirement is that it be a
wholesome or neutral object, not one that triggers any feelings of attachment
or anger or views that undermine the keys. In other words, it's best not to
choose your lover or your boss whom you dislike. The idea is to learn to
concentrate on that object for longer and longer periods of time, without
other thoughts intervening, until you can stay with it effortlessly. The easiest
object to start with is your own breath, which is why this meditation is
regularly taught in beginner's classes.

Learning concentration meditation is not a mystical undertaking. It's not even that difficult. It just takes time, effort and an ability to deal with some frustration while you get the hang of it. The rewards are worth it. Not only do you learn to focus and concentrate on the Buddha's teachings, you'll also reap tremendous side benefits. To begin with, concentration meditation is a great stress reliever. It lowers your blood pressure and combats depression and other emotional problems. It makes your mind more serene and peaceful, and your relationships improve because of this. The original interpretation of the fifth key is 'to remain in peace'.

Concentration meditation can also be intensely pleasurable. Once you learn to hold the object of concentration, you'll experience both harmony and pleasure in your body and mind. Mind pleasure makes your mind tremendously joyful, happy, peaceful and satisfied. Body pleasure makes your body feel very light and light-filled. This may sound like the kind of pleasure you can get from alcohol or recreational drugs. The difference with meditation is that you are in control, and it won't lead to a hangover or any negative side effects. Some say that meditation is better than sex, but you'll have to decide.

All these benefits are fantastic and it's wonderful to enjoy them, but remember your ultimate aim. When you're learning concentration meditation in the context of the six keys, your goal is to cut the root of your suffering and gain enlightenment. You want to be able to focus and concentrate so you that you can practise analytical meditation: the ability to think about and analyze the information the Buddha shared with a stable, clear and lucid mind. You want to understand and realize unlimited compassion and wisdom, because doing this will set you free. When you achieve that ultimate state of happiness, you'll be able to love and care for others without limit. You will also be free from fear and negativity of all kinds. There is no greater happiness than this.

CREATE YOUR MEDITATION SPACE

You could just sit down anywhere and start meditating on your breath, but it helps to create a separate place for meditation — one that is sacred and special and supports your practice.

MAKE YOUR MEDITATION SPACE SACRED

The ideal space is a spare room that you can give over entirely to meditation, but most likely you'll need to create your meditation space in the corner of your bedroom or another functioning room. Consider this place sacred and different from the rest of your living space — a place dedicated to your meditation practice. You may want to use a screen to separate your meditation corner from the rest of the room. If you don't have the room to spare, create a temporary sacred space that can be put away when not in use. Always meditating in the same space, although not necessary, supports your practice. When you enter your sacred space, it's a signal to your mind and heart that you're about to meditate.

The Buddha suggested that you choose a quiet, clean, healthy space that is free from danger. In other words, don't try to meditate in a room filled with mould or paint fumes, or with a television blaring in the background, or in a house in a dangerous neighbourhood. The Buddha taught in India 2,500 years ago, so his examples would have been different: 'dangers' then may have been thieves or tigers, and the health issues may have been of the sanitary variety. What you want is as serene and safe a place as possible. If you live with someone, hopefully he or she will be supportive of your meditation practice. Even if your meditation space is less than optimal, it's always better to meditate than not.

Clean your new meditation space thoroughly. Vacuum and dust and, if you have a floor you can mop, do so. This isn't simply to create a tidy space. It's to clear negative energy from yourself, as well as from your environment. For this reason, try to do a little cleaning before every meditation session.

Sit down and make sure you feel comfortable in the place you've chosen. Is the air fresh? Are there any draughts? Is the lighting pleasant? If you live with other people, make sure you have created adequate privacy.

GATHER YOUR MEDITATION KIT

Now that you've created and prepared your sacred space for meditation, you need something to sit on. If you're comfortable having one, an altar will help you remember the sacredness of meditation and your intention to become enlightened. A bell will help you begin and end your meditation session. Comfortable clothing and blankets or shawls for additional warmth will help you sit for longer periods.

TAKE YOUR SEAT

The Buddha recommended sitting cross-legged on the ground or floor on a soft cushion of some kind. You can use an ordinary cushion, but you may want to consider buying one made especially for meditation. You can find them online or at meditation centres. They come in all shapes, sizes and colours, and may be stuffed with a variety of materials, including kapok and buckwheat shells. Some are even adjustable. If possible, try them out first and see what feels best to you.

You may want to invest in a larger flat mat called a *zabuton* to go under your cushion. This serves to raise you a little higher off the ground and also protects your ankles. You can also buy smaller support cushions to place under your knees or ankles if you experience pain in these areas.

If you have trouble sitting in the traditional way, you can meditate on any straight-backed chair. Some companies have recently started selling specialist 'meditation chairs', which fall somewhere between a normal chair and a cushion. They give you back support and you can sit on them cross-legged if you choose. Another popular device, called a 'backjack', supports your back while allowing you to sit on the floor in the traditional style. There are a variety of these back-support devices available.

CREATE AN ALTAR

Consider creating a small altar on top of a low table or chest of drawers. If you like, cover the surface with a special cloth. Add an image or statue of the Buddha or another inspirational figure. If you're not comfortable with that, add objects from nature you find inspiring — perhaps a beautiful crystal, a special stone or a shell. Then add offerings such as a candle, a small bowl of water, incense, flowers or fruit. Consider these substances as symbolic of a vast array of gifts and treasures offered to your higher power, whomever or whatever that may be. You make offerings to the Buddha, Christ or your higher power in order to connect to their energy and obtain blessings. You can also make offerings to yourself as your own future buddha.

WEAR COMFORTABLE CLOTHES

Your clothing should be clean and loose fitting. You don't need anything special, just something comfortable. Because you could be sitting for long periods of time, you may want warm socks and a shawl or blanket of some kind.

CLASSICAL 7-POINT MEDITATION POSTURE

Start by sitting comfortably on a cushion on the floor, and then arrange your body according to the seven points listed below.

1 Your spine, from the nape of your neck to the small of the back, should be as straight as possible without being rigid. Imagine a pile of coins stacked on top of one another.

2 Your legs are crossed. Your right leg is drawn over your left leg. The backs of your feet sit flat on the tops of your thighs. Ideally, your two feet make a straight line.

3 Your shoulders are even and relaxed. Try not to sit with one shoulder higher than the other.

4 Your chin is parallel with the floor and tucked in slightly.

5 Your eyes are relaxed, open and slightly lowered. Look into the space around one metre (three feet) in front, at nothing in particular.

6 Your tongue is placed against your upper palate.

7 Your lips are slightly parted, and your teeth are touching but not clenched. You're breathing through your nose.

BEGIN AND END WITH A BELL

You may want to buy a small bell or a small set of Tibetan Buddhist cymbals called *tingshas* to mark the beginning and end of your meditation sessions. A beautiful sound will help you create sacred space and focus your mind.

LEARN HOW TO SIT

Whether you sit in a chair or on a cushion, it's important to keep your spine straight. It should not be tight and rigid, but rather lifted upward, as if a string is pulling you up from the crown of your head. Your chest should be open and relaxed. Keeping your back straight, your shoulders level and your chest open allows energy and breath to flow freely. If you can cross your legs, that's great, but it's not essential for practising concentration meditation. Your chin should be parallel with the floor, not jutting out or pulled back too far. Your eyes should be open, cast downward and focused about one metre (three feet) in front of you.

One of the challenges of concentration meditation is to be able to sit for long periods of time without getting so uncomfortable you feel you need to stop. Stay aware of your body throughout your meditation session and make micro-adjustments to prevent your muscles from cramping or your feet from falling asleep. If you need to, stretch your legs, adjust your posture and then start again. With practice, sitting in meditation becomes easier.

Try out the classical 7-point meditation posture (see opposite) before you actually start to meditate. You may discover you need extra padding under your ankles or knees. If so, use small pillows to prop them up. If you've chosen to sit in a straight-backed chair, practise sitting up straight, feet on the floor. Sit without touching the back of the chair.

PREPARE YOUR MIND AND HEART

The Buddha made four suggestions to help you prepare for meditation practice. First, to help your concentration he suggested removing as many distractions from your life as possible. To do this, he recommended you live a simple life and be content with what you have. The less you have the less you have to work for and manage.

Second, if you're caught up in a lot of activities — the busy-lazy syndrome — he recommended cutting back as much as possible so you can devote more time to meditation. If you find you are unable to sit still and always have to be on the run, it may take you a while to wean yourself off the need for frantic activity.

Third, the Buddha suggested that you review the second key, Do no harm. In order to keep your thoughts and behaviour as pure as possible, you need to cut back on your desires. It's easier said than done, but if you can reduce your desire for fame or status or this person or that possession, you'll cut

down on your mental agitation, which will increase your ability to practise concentration meditation.

Finally, before you begin a meditation session, set your motivation. Aspire to practise concentration meditation in order to free yourself and all other beings from suffering, and deliver yourself and them to enlightenment. That's a lofty ideal, and at this point may not be as compelling as all the other great benefits, such as being better at your job, relieving stress and experiencing great pleasure. It's fine to meditate in order to gain these more immediate rewards, but when you practise concentration meditation as one of Buddha's keys, it's important to keep the highest motivation in the forefront of your mind. The other benefits will follow naturally.

BREATH MEDITATION

You can meditate on any object, such as an image of the Buddha or a candle, as long as it's positive or neutral. But it's good to start learning concentration by meditating on your breath, because it's always with you. Meditating on an object or your breath gives your mind something to 'hang on to' when it starts to jump from one thought to another. Training your mind in this way helps you focus on one thing at a time and develop your powers of concentration.

Find a quiet time where you can be undisturbed in your meditation space for about half an hour. Tidy up the space and mentally imagine clearing away any obstacles to learning to concentrate. Get comfortable on your cushion or straight-backed chair. Go over the classical 7-point posture and approximate it as best as you can. Be sure to keep your back straight, your shoulders level and relaxed, and your chin parallel to the floor. Lower your eyes and focus about one metre (three feet) in front of you. Let your hands rest gently on your knees or cradle your right hand in your left and let them rest gently in your lap.

Take a moment to set your motivation. Offer this meditation session for the benefit of yourself and all sentient beings.

Begin breathing normally through your nose, using your abdomen rather than your chest. Don't force your breath or breathe noisily. Just let it go in and out freely. Check your posture and relax any part of your body that is tense. If you have a small bell or *tingshas*, ring it when you feel ready to start your meditation session.

Focus on your breath by counting each exhalation and when you reach ten, begin again. Try to be totally focused on your breath and the sensation of it passing through your nostrils, down into your belly and back again. Thoughts and feelings will intervene but when they do, simply let them go and return to counting your breath. Be gentle with yourself as you would with a small child who has strayed. Regardless of how many times it happens, just return to your breath. After about 15 minutes, end your meditation session by ringing your bell or *tingshas*.

If possible, start to meditate on a daily basis for 15 minutes a day. Pick a time that will work for you and try to develop a steady, consistent practice.

THINGS TO DO

By noting where your mind takes you geographically, this exercise will help you appreciate how your mind continuously jumps from one thought to another. Begin your session as you did for the breath meditation, but this time have pencil and paper in hand so you can jot things down. Try to avoid all thoughts by concentrating only on your breath. Count on the in-breath from one to ten and start over when you reach ten. When a thought crosses your mind, make a note of where you were geographically. If you were thinking about something at home, write 'home'; if it was to do with shopping, write down the location of the shop. If your mind wanders to another city or country, note that as well. After ten minutes, end your meditation and review your list. Where has your mind travelled?

OBSTACLES TO MEDITATION

It's inevitable that you will have difficulties when you first begin to meditate. It sounds so simple but you'll be amazed at how difficult it is to stay focused on a single object. No matter how hard you try, your thoughts will intervene.

Then your knees or back start hurting, or you may get bored and want to stop after only a few minutes. Some people experience an unexpected emotional reaction and feel angry or afraid.

Don't give up. Rest assured that if you develop a consistent meditation practice, these problems will recede and your meditation will become joyful and fulfilling. With time and practice, you'll begin to reap the benefits of learning to concentrate.

To help you through the initial frustration, let's look at some of the most common problems and how to deal with them.

LAZINESS

This is the most common obstacle to learning to meditate. It's difficult to add something new to an already busy life and when you feel a time crunch, meditation can be the first thing to go. The antidote to laziness is the joy and pleasure that your meditation will eventually provide. When you reach this point, you find yourself feeling cranky if you have to miss even one day. But since that pleasure takes a while to develop, at the outset you'll have to remind yourself of the benefits concentration meditation will ultimately bring, and look forward to using your newfound powers of concentration in all areas of your life. Go back and review the fourth key, Sweat it out, and let your enthusiasm inspire your practice.

FORGETTING THE OBJECT OF YOUR MEDITATION

Sometimes you can completely forget the object you are meditating on. You may find, for example, that after a short time you've completely forgotten to focus on your breath. Mindfulness, the kind you practised when washing the dishes, is the antidote. In your everyday life, forgetfulness is the biggest cause of accidents. Daydreaming your way into a car accident is a perfect example. Burning your dinner is another. Whenever you realize you've completely lost your focus on your breath, try to bring mindfulness to your practice. You accomplish this by watching your focus out of one corner of your mind's eye.

A SINKING, WANDERING OR EXCITED MIND

These three obstacles all weaken your focus and concentration. 'Sinking' basically refers to falling asleep. Sinking in a more subtle form is a focus that lacks clarity, as if you're holding a cup so loosely in your hand it will eventually slip from your grip. If you feel the need to stop your meditation session, get some fresh air and start again.

A wandering mind is fairly self-explanatory, describing a tendency to move frequently between thoughts or memories. A subtle form of wandering is focusing on your breath while simultaneously thinking of something else. To correct this, devote a part of your mind to observing how your meditation is progressing so that you can make corrections and achieve mental clarity and alertness.

The third obstacle is excitement or an intense desire or craving for something or someone. The most frequent distractions in meditation are caused by desire and attachment – perhaps thinking about your lover or a favourite dessert. Like sinking and wandering, excitement is cured by installing a monitor in a corner of your mind to keep you on track.

NOT CORRECTING PROBLEMS AS THEY ARISE

Continuing to meditate without correcting problems will hinder your progress. The problems will multiply and you'll eventually put a stop to your meditation practice out of frustration.

BEING HARD ON YOURSELF

Learning to focus and concentrate takes patience. Don't correct yourself to the point where you feel oppressed and discouraged. Balance is the key. If you have a steady and consistent meditation practice, correct problems as they arise but also have compassion for yourself, you'll make great progress.

KEY **6**

GET REAL

In the previous chapter, you learned about the fifth key, Stick to the point, or how to practise concentration meditation. If you really work at concentration meditation, you will achieve what is called 'calm abiding': a wonderful, peaceful state that creates harmony within both your body and mind. Tibetan Buddhist masters describe this pleasure as a feeling of warmth spreading throughout the body, combined with the sensation of being as light as a feather. Eventually, you develop a sense of inseparability from the object on which you are meditating. You may even feel as though your body disappears and that you are flying. At this point you have achieved tremendous stability and clarity, can fix your mind on any topic and meditate for as long as you want.

Having this powerful, stable, lucid and pleasurable state of mind helps you meditate on and understand the first four keys. Unfortunately, unless you cut through the root of your unhappiness, life then intervenes, and you eventually fall from this blissful state. Rather than just enjoy your ability to meditate and develop, the Buddha recommended using your powers of concentration to end your suffering once and for all. The sixth key, Get real, will help you use meditation to begin to understand the true nature of reality, which will lead you eventually to wisdom and enlightenment.

It's important to recognize that enlightenment is a profound state and an extraordinary achievement, and this very brief introduction to the Buddha's keys cannot possibly deliver that. If you are truly motivated to pursue the

Buddha's path, it is best to find a qualified teacher who can help you complete your journey. But, that said, there's a lot you can do to get a headstart on understanding wisdom and ending your suffering. Just casting doubt on the way you usually see things will set you on your way. That little bit of doubt can topple the house of cards that is your mistaken notion of reality and the source of your delusions and your suffering.

The Buddha taught that even if you don't fully realize wisdom or become enlightened, just a partial understanding of how reality works can deliver more happiness in this life and a better rebirth in your next. This chapter introduces some questions and alternative views about how people and things actually exist and how they really function. We'll also look at the way in which the conventional means of perceiving reality perpetuates suffering.

A famous Indian Buddhist master Chandrakirti, who lived in the seventh century told the following story about the power of a little doubt:

A sea captain was once captured by a monster, who held him prisoner on an island and warned him never to venture to the island's south side. Finally, one day when the monster was taking a nap, the captain defied her order and slipped off to explore. Waiting for him on the other side of the island was a beautiful, magnificent steed known as Balahaka, the king of horses. The captain was wise enough to know that if he could hold on to just one hair of Balahaka's mane, the horse would carry him across the ocean to the safety of the other shore. So, by grabbing on to just one hair, he escaped his suffering and set himself free.

By beginning to question how you habitually view reality, you too can grab on to a hair of Balahaka's mane.

THE TRUTHS WILL SET YOU FREE

When the Buddha achieved enlightenment, he wanted to let others know that they could accomplish the same. The first thing he shared was his discovery of what is known as the Four Noble Truths:

All life is suffering

Your suffering is caused by your attachment, anger and ignorance

You can end your suffering

There is a path you can follow to accomplish this

We've talked about suffering, and how no matter how good it gets, our lives remain unsatisfactory and fail to deliver ultimate happiness. In Let it go, Bite your tongue, Do no harm and Sweat it out, we talked about our delusions and how we keep generating negative karma, and suffering the karmic consequences in life after life. We've talked about how the Buddha said it is possible to achieve enlightenment and end this merry-go-round of endless dissatisfaction. And we've been working on the keys as a path toward that enlightenment.

The good news is that you've learned ways to generate virtue and reduce your negativity. But if you're going to achieve ultimate happiness, you have to cut your delusions out completely. The sixth key explores the Buddha's Third Noble Truth: that it is possible to end suffering by eliminating our mistaken view of reality — the jet engine that powers our delusions. We 'get real' by waking up to the true way we, others and things exist and function.

OUR BIGGEST PROBLEM

The fact is that we project a false way of existing on others, ourselves and things. We do this by mentally creating a solid, concrete, separate and static reality, when in truth, 'reality' is a dynamic collection of interdependent and transitory phenomena. The Buddha called this idea 'dependent arising': the notion that anything you look at is a collection of parts that are constantly changing, rather than a single unitary thing. Buddhists call waking up to how things really are as 'understanding emptiness'. It doesn't mean that people and things are empty in the sense of non-existence. Rather, emptiness means that we and they are 'empty' of the false separateness and solidity we've been projecting on to them life after life. It's this mistaken understanding of how people and things exist and function that causes us to suffer.

If you experience yourself as a solid, separate 'I' and, by extension, the most important person in your universe, you're automatically courting conflict and delusions. 'I' gives rise to 'my' and 'mine', and soon you have 'my' house, 'my' partner, 'my' food, when in fact you can't really find the 'my' in any of them. This possessive and self-cherishing mind that projects solidity and separateness on everything and everyone gives rise to jealousy, meanness and even hatred.

When you label someone else's behaviour a 'problem', you're mentally creating something solid 'out there', when the 'problem' resides in the thoughts and projections of your mind. This isn't to say that person *isn't* behaving in a certain way — but how you view and experience him or her makes all the difference to your level of happiness. Another example is developing attachment to and desire for a new car: projecting status, pleasure and happiness on to what is literally a bunch of inert parts. Does this mean that you shouldn't enjoy a new car? No. It means understanding that pleasure and happiness don't reside in the car, but are in your mind and the way in which you view reality.

DEVELOPING COMPASSION MEDITATION

When I have a strong sense of a solid 'I', I feel that I am the most important person. Accompanying my strong self-cherishing comes 'my'. I have strong attachments to 'my' parents, 'my' partner, 'my' children and 'my' friends. Not only am I most important in my world, so are all my nearest and dearest.

But when I challenge my strong sense of a solid 'I', I notice I experience less conflict with others. I begin to feel that more people are loveable — even those I previously had difficulty with or didn't know. I see how everyone is suffering and wants to be happy, and in that way they are no different from me. I know firsthand how they are suffering from jealousy, anger, fear and rigid ideas about reality, and my heart goes out to them.

It's becoming more difficult to see myself or my dear ones as more important than others. I'm even beginning to see that everyone's needs are

equal. I'm not there yet, but it may eventually dawn on me that the needs of others are actually *more* important than mine. These are the Buddha's teachings on equanimity.

I'm happy my heart is opening and I pray that my compassion for myself and others continues to grow.

LOOKING UNDER REALITY'S HOOD

You can begin to glimpse the Buddha's discoveries about how phenomena truly exist if you combine the powers of concentration you learned about in the last chapter with analytical meditation, and begin to examine your assumptions about yourself, others and things. This is a kind of meditative detective work. You begin to search for the solid, static and separate entities you have been so convinced exist.

The Buddha recommended you start investigating people and things in three ways: by looking at the causes of their existence and how they're interconnected with everything else; by looking at their parts; and by looking at how you think about and label them.

HOW DID THIS PIECE OF PAPER COME TO BE?

Thich Nhat Hanh, a famous contemporary Buddhist teacher, likes to use a simple piece of paper as an example. In the piece of paper you can find the earth, a seed, the tree, the sunshine, the clouds, the rain, the logger who cut down the tree, the workers at the mill who made the wood into paper, the distributor who packaged it and got it to a shop, and the salesperson who sold it to you. This simple piece of paper is a collection of many causes and conditions coming together. The tree, the rainstorm, the logger are no longer in the paper, so once you have the result —

the piece of paper — the causes and conditions are long gone. It's easy to forget or even fail to realize they were once there.

The example of a simple piece of paper drives home the fact that things are not separate and permanent, but are the result of many causes and conditions that you can trace back to infinity. But in our mind we forget the dizzying array of causes and conditions and interconnections and just skip to the idea of a solid, separate, static piece of paper. In reality, the paper doesn't exist in that way. Even as we hold it in our hands, its atoms are in constant motion. The light and air are acting on it and causing subtle deterioration. It's also interacting with our bodies, which are in a state of constant change.

116

WHAT PART OF THE CLOCK IS THE CLOCK?

The second way to counter our mistaken notion of the solidity and separateness of things is to look at their parts. Take the example of a clock. It's a solid object that seems to exist separately from everything else. But what if you take the clock apart and lay out all the hundreds of pieces on a table? Where's the clock now? Is it in the clock's face, the hands, the gears, the plastic, the metal or the alarm? Now start thinking about the causes and conditions behind each part as you did for the piece of paper. How did the metal in the clock or the printed clock face come to be? You'll begin to appreciate that solid, separate clock is really a dynamic, interconnected collection of parts, which have come together as the result of many different factors.

The habit of projecting on to people and things a solid, separate and unchanging reality fuels our delusions of anger, hatred, jealousy and desire that cause us so much unhappiness. Next time you feel yourself becoming

obsessed with an expensive work suit you can't afford but which you imagine will enhance your sex appeal and career success, spend some time meditating on its causes, conditions and parts. Imagine it showing wear over time and see yourself eventually throwing it away. In the short term, this approach may seem to take the air out of your enjoyment of life. But if you understand the real nature of a suit, you'll be able to enjoy the ones you wear even more, because you'll have a realistic view of what a suit is: a combination of cloth, buttons, zip, thread and padding — that you have temporary use of. You won't get hysterical if someone spills something on 'your' expensive suit, and you won't expect it to deliver ultimate happiness. You'll be happier and more at peace, because your relationship to people and things will be congruent with how they actually are, not what you perceive them to be.

WHAT'S IN A NAME?

The next thing to consider is the way in which everything exists for you through the filter of your mind, which identifies whatever your eyes see through a process of labelling. Before you call something a piece of paper, a clock or a suit, it isn't any of those things. As we've discussed, these apparently solid items are constantly changing collections of interconnected parts, which result from a myriad of causes and conditions. Your mind lumps all those parts and qualities together, gives them a label and thereby makes each appear to be something that is separate and distinct.

We need to label things in order to communicate with each other in daily life. Otherwise, how would we be able to take a bus, order something in a restaurant or ask someone the time? It's vital to have everyday conventions we more or less agree on. The problem is we don't stop at practical labels. We begin to see all the things we label as permanent, solid and separate, and we begin to mistake our thoughts and feelings about others as reality. This one is an enemy, that one a friend. We actually believe our labels, which further supports our view of others as separate and different. This undermines our ability to develop love and compassion. We forget that, in fact, we are intimately connected with everyone and everything on the planet.

WHAT MAKES A HUMAN BEING?

We've talked mostly about *things*, but the Buddha's discoveries also apply to people. Like a piece of paper, a clock or a suit, we are not solid, separate or permanent. It's that strong feeling of 'I' that gets us into trouble. We need to examine that notion in more detail, but first let's look at the way in which the Buddha described the nature of human existence.

The Buddha came up with a scheme of five collections, or 'aggregates', that combine together to make up a human being: your body, your senses, your conceptions, your will and your consciousness. Think of the first and last as your body and mind, and the other three as the activities that occur within them.

YOUR BODY

The Buddha described your body as 'a bubble in water'. It looks big and solid but, like a bubble, if you make a little hole in it, it goes. That's how fragile your body is.

YOUR SENSES

He then described your six senses: eyes, ears, nose, tongue, body and brain. Why the brain? Because it senses memories and emotions that are produced

internally and generates dreams. The Buddha emphasized that the physical
and mental sensations you experience as emotions depend on how you
perceive and react to others, your environment and your own thoughts.
Your mental and emotional suffering is often a result of how you perceive
the world.

YOUR CONCEPTIONS

The Buddha described your conceptions of the world as 'a magician's show'.
This is where we have our problems with projection and mistaken notions
about reality. Conceptions are mental ideas we construct out of our sensory
perceptions. For instance, there are a millions of colours and hues, but our
minds pull together a bunch of them that fall within a certain range and give
them a single name, like 'blue'. Our ability to generalize and label helps us
function on a day-to-day basis, but we mistakenly go beyond that and believe
our conceptualizations and labels are 'real'.

JOURNAL EXERCISE

We experience the false, solid sense of 'I' most acutely when someone accuses us of doing something we didn't do. Imagine you're in a supermarket minding your own business and someone starts pointing at you and yelling loudly that you are a thief. Your response will likely be embarrassment, anger and outrage that you've been wrongly accused.

But if you look at the scene objectively, someone is just yelling loudly and pointing at you. Your sense that you exist solidly and separately from everyone and everything else is what has triggered your negative emotions. If you didn't feel that big solid 'I' rise up against the person accusing you, you would have a better chance of resolving the situation with compassion and without negativity.

Write about situations in which you were wrongly accused and describe how you reacted. If you had a different view of yourself and how you existed in the world, would you have reacted differently?

YOUR WILL

Your will is the function of your mind that results in mental, verbal and physical acts. It's the source impulse that creates your karma.

YOUR CONSCIOUSNESS

Your consciousness or your mind itself, manifests in your constant thinking process. The Buddha divided your consciousness into six different types, depending on which of the six senses it relies on to function.

WILL THE REAL 'ME' STAND UP?

In order to find out if we exist in the solid, separate way we think we do, the Buddha came up with a systematic 7-point exercise. It's based on the five aggregates or parts which we just covered.

1 Which one of my parts is 'me'? Am I my body? Am I my feelings? Am I my concepts? Am I my actions? Am I my consciousness? The answer is that none of them, separately, is really 'me'.

2 Am 'I' separate from my parts? Am I floating out there, separate from my body, my feelings, my concepts, my actions and my consciousness? No, that doesn't ring true.

3 Am 'I' part of all my parts? Am 'I' part of my body, my feelings, my concepts, my actions and my consciousness? No, because this is like saying when 'I' ride a horse, I become a man-horse or woman-horse — a part of the horse, like a centaur. It sounds promising at first, but it doesn't work.

4 Can I put 'me' on my parts, like fruit on a plate? No, because then there would be two things: 'me' and my parts.

5 Can my parts be put on 'me'? Again, this is supposing two separate things, not one.

6 Am 'I' my actual shape or form? Is that my real 'self'? Good try, but if this is true, then my 'self' would be only a physical thing, as my mind and feelings have no shape.

7 Am 'I' the combination of all my parts? No, because in this scenario, with my parts all lumped together, there would be no need or room for 'I'.

This exercise demonstrates a search for an inherently existent, solid 'self' or 'I'. We have an idea that we exist inherently, independently, even permanently. Upon examination, we see that we cannot possibly exist in this way.

So how do you exist? You are a combination of your aggregates, the causes and conditions that brought you into being (your karma and physical parents), and the label by which you can be recognized. In this way you are able to function happily and continue. But when we examine our experience, we see that there is no solid little being inside us to whom our experience refers. Joseph Goldstein, another contemporary Buddhist teacher, compares our existence to that of a rainbow:

We go out after a rainstorm and feel that moment of delight if a rainbow appears in the sky. Mostly, we simply enjoy the sight without investigating the real nature of what is happening. But when we look more deeply, it becomes clear that there is no 'thing' called 'rainbow' apart from the particular conditions of air and moisture and light. Each one of us is like that rainbow — an appearance, a magical display, arising out of our various elements of mind and body.

Originally quoted in 'Dharma 101', Tricycle: The Buddhist Review, Vol. VI, #3.

If you do the 7-point meditation at a deeper level, you'll feel a very powerful shift in the way you view reality. If you do it over and over, you'll begin to see that you, others and things exist in a conventional way, but are not absolute, solid or separate. This is the beginning of the end of your painful and afflicted emotions. No longer will you think on the lines of 'How could he do that to me?', 'I should be treated better!' or 'That's mine!' Your selfish grasping will loosen and you'll be more naturally at ease with everyone and everything. You'll be satisfied with things just as they are. And, self-hating references about yourself such as 'I'm terrible' or 'I blew it' will dissipate.

When you get frightened or upset, ask yourself who it is that is frightened. Who is the one who can't manage, can't function or can't take it? If these feelings arise and you have even a little doubt about your separate, inherent existence, your sense of hurt, anger and fear will dissolve right then and there! This is the power of a little doubt, or grabbing on to just one hair of Balahaka's mane. Finally, you can begin to relax. That little doubt may eventually set you free.

PRAYER: THE FOUR IMMEASURABLES

May all beings have happiness and the causes of happiness.
May all beings be free from suffering and the causes of suffering.
May all beings never be separated from freedom's true joy.
May all beings dwell in equanimity, free from attachment and aversion.

INDEX

ACKNOWLEDGEMENTS

Alamy/Creatas 102 bottom; /James Dawson 109 main; /Garry Gay 29 main; /Goodshoot 57 bottom. **Corbis UK Limited**/15 top left; /Yann Arthus-Bertrand 100 bottom; /Phil Banko 82 centre left; /Dennis Degnan 119 top; /Jon Feingersh 17 bottom; /Werner Forman 73 bottom right; /Rick Gomez 34 centre left; /Steve Kaufman 86 bottom; /Thom Lang 52 centre left; /Laureen March 65 main; /David A. Northcott 36 bottom right; /Keren Su 23 bottom right; /LWA-Stephen Welstead 26 main. **Getty Images**/James Baigrie 35 bottom right; /Martin Barraud 113 top left; /Steve Bly 19 centre right; /Roy Botterell 16 top right; /Paul Cherfils 116 bottom; /Color Day Production 60 bottom right; /Paul Dance 32 bottom left; /Peter Dazeley 79 main; /Josef Fankhauser 22 centre left; /Kevin Fitzgerald 91 centre right, 114 top; /Michael Goldman 50 bottom left; /Dan Ham 83 bottom right; /Howard Huang 53 centre left; /Mike Kelly 18 bottom right; /Clarissa Leahy 106 main; /Peter Mason 76 bottom; /John & Lisa Merrill 8 bottom left; /Kelvin Murray 59 centre right; /Stan Osolinski 103 centre right; /Peter Scholey 98 bottom right; /Stephen Simpson 20 top; /Hugh Sitton 12-13 bottom; /Harry Taylor 70 bottom; /Paul Thomas 39 centre right, 47 bottom left; /Michele Westmorland 55 top; /Mark Williams 51 main; /Yellow Dog Productions 96 top. **Octopus Publishing Group Limited**/5 background, 6 centre left, 7 top, 9 bottom right, 11 main, 14 centre right, 25 top, 31 main, 43 main, 44 bottom left, 46 centre left, 48 top, 58 main, 62-63 bottom, 69 main, 80 top right, 81 bottom right, 85 top, 87 bottom right, 99 top right, 105 bottom, 110 bottom, 115 bottom right, 117 bottom right, 120 main, 123 top, 125 main; /Mike Hemsley at Walter Gardiner Photography 37 Background; /Ian Parsons 97 bottom; /Stephen Conroy 72 top right; /Peter Myers 75 bottom, 94 bottom right; /Peter Pugh Cook 89 main; /William Reavell 67 bottom right, 84 bottom left; /Russell Sadur 45 bottom right; /Unit Photographic 41 centre right; /Ian Wallace 92 bottom; /Mark Winwood 61 bottom, 74 bottom right.

Executive Editor Brenda Rosen
Managing Editor Clare Churly
Executive Art Editor Sally Bond
Designer Pia Ingham and Lloyd Tilbury for Cobalt Id
Picture Library Manager Jennifer Veall
Production Manager Louise Hall